THE MARKETER'S
PLAYBOOK

The CMO's Guide to Modern Marketing

Tony Quin

Press

The Marketer's Playbook
The CMO's Guide to Modern Marketing

Copyright © 2018 by Tony Quin
All rights reserved.

For information on SoDA Press visit:
www.sodaspeaks.com

ISBN: 978-0-9998585-0-9

Design by Alan Barnett
Cover illustration by Carol Montoto

Thank you to my wonderful wife, LouAnn, and all the others who have patiently endured the process of my writing this book. Thanks also to my parents for putting marketing in my DNA, and my colleagues, clients, and friends without whom I wouldn't have had anything to write about.

— *Tony Quin*

CONTENTS

CONNECTING THE DOTS

What's changed, how it will affect you, and what you can do about it

It used to be that "considered purchases" were anything really expensive, complex, or difficult to understand—purchases, like cars, that required buyers to invest time and trouble to research. But consumers now have enormous digital power at their fingertips, which means that virtually any purchase can easily be explored, weighed, compared and carefully considered. As a result, buyers now treat most products like considered purchases.

This book presents solutions to this and other marketing challenges ushered in by the digital age. It's designed for people who recognize that smart marketing and a consumer-centric approach are critical to the success of any business in our post-advertising world. While big brands are, for the most part, already adapting to the new dynamics, most smaller companies are still trying to figure out a game plan. Just throwing money at the problem, the way their larger cousins can, is not an option. That's why this book gives company leaders a step-by-step guide for how to build a comprehensive modern marketing system that's designed to attract, retain and grow digitally savvy customers. For the first time, technology combined with consumer insights can give companies the ability to have one-to-one relationships that can take their brands to the next level.

"The Marketer's Playbook" focuses on the fundamentals that will power marketing for years to come.

But first, let's all get on the same page about the word "marketing," a term bandied about with impunity, and with no small measure of confusion. For the purposes of this book, marketing means anything and everything that touches the consumer. This covers all that a company does to get, keep and grow customers. It incorporates many consumer touchpoints that in the past might have been considered out of the marketing arena, but in our new consumer-centric world have become critical influencers of consumer attitudes.

These changes to the world of marketing are only one of the many transformations brought on by computing and the internet. In the last twenty years, those of us toiling in the marketing trenches have watched commerce being reinvented, piece by piece. Along the way we've tried to understand what's changing and what's not, and how all the pieces fit together. We've also tried to explain to the people who run companies what they need to do to adapt. Now, as the impact of digital on how people buy and marketers sell seems clear to everyone, the time is right for a book that connects the dots and outlines how to build a modern marketing system that will help your business succeed in this new reality.

While there are countless whitepapers, articles and books that dive with excruciating detail into the weeds of this new marketing landscape, the problem for most business leaders is seeing the big picture, so they can chart the right course for the future. If you are running a company, you need a new approach to consumers, and you need to be able to lead your team to get it done. That's why this book focuses on the fundamentals that will power commerce for the foreseeable future. These are not the trendy technology innovations that explode onto the scene and often quickly fade away; they are the structural dynamics of the digitally shaped marketplace that are unlikely to change soon. Our goal with this book is to provide you with an action plan for how to construct a modern marketing system for this new marketplace. It's not a detailed blueprint, but rather a bird's eye view of the whole forest, which will enable company leaders to see what's important and how all the pieces need to work together.

THE GREAT RECESSION

Companies of all sizes, but especially smaller companies, pulled in their horns and their toes out of the internet water.

In order to understand where we are today, it helps to understand where we have come from. This doesn't require the entire history of marketing, but rather just an understanding of what's changed recently, since the attitudes and mind-sets that drove that period still linger.

Before the Great Recession, many companies were focused on building out the technology to make their production and supply chains more efficient. A great deal of money was spent to squeeze costs and improve systems efficiency. Then around 2003, the internet really started to kick in as broadband proliferated. Consumers were intrigued, and early-adopter companies jumped in to experiment. By 2008, the internet was already in second gear. Fortune 100 companies were fully committed and shifted their already powerful marketing organizations to take advantage of the new opportunities. But most midsize companies still held back. Despite being on everybody's lips, the internet had not yet changed everything.

Then the recession hit. Companies of all sizes, but especially smaller companies, pulled in their horns and their toes out of the internet water. By 2009, according to the National Association of Advertisers, 93% of members cited cost-cutting. It was a challenging time, and the first thing to be cut was often anything unproven and experimental. Most of corporate America slowed down. But a funny thing happened—consumers *didn't* slow down; their digital adoption didn't stop for a second. They couldn't get enough of all things digital and the rate of technological adoption just kept accelerating. Large companies, with their deep pockets already laser-focused on their consumers, stayed right there with them and kept innovating and investing.

THE FAT PART OF THE SNAKE

As 2015 dawned...the late majority, the fat part of the snake, which waited out the recession, woke up to a new reality.

Seven years later, as 2015 dawned, companies looked around and finally felt firm footing. As they surveyed the scene, they also saw a radically transformed environment. They saw a different consumer, empowered by new technology, confident and hungry for more. Gone were the AOL training wheels. Now with search, social media, and cheap broadband, consumers were technically savvy, independent and powerful. And so, companies in "the late majority" (the fat part of the snake, which had waited out the recession and resisted change) woke up to the new reality.

The profound shift that had happened was in the transfer of power from companies to consumers made possible by the internet. Where companies had been able to use information, distance and time to manage consumers in the past, in this new internet-fueled world these controls had quickly faded. Now consumers could not only find out where and when to get the best price, but which product was superior and why, all without leaving the comfort of their living room. The internet in all its forms had completely redefined how consumers discover, evaluate, buy and experience products and services. Along the way this seismic shift had also left much of the old marketing paradigm in the rubble.

THE NEW BOSS

Companies have no choice but to super-serve their consumers.

Marketing used to mean mostly paid advertising; ads in print and TV and other traditional channels, which had the job of getting awareness, making the pitch and often closing the deal. Consumers were pretty much captive audiences; you couldn't fast forward through the TV commercials or block out ads with your ad blocker. Today, however, consumers, trained to be expert digital buyers, expect to be in charge. They value input and advice from brands, but they are going to make up their own minds. Consumers are the new boss and they know it. That's why companies have no choice but to super-serve them with excellent products and value that stand up to scrutiny.

The new marketing is not just advertising, but everything that touches your consumer. Every time a brand interacts with a prospect or a customer, from the first time they hear your name to the moment they become your most loyal fan, it's marketing. It's a value chain, which brings the promise and meaning of your brand to life. It's what sets your brand and company apart from the competition, and it's the way to build long-term loyalty and value.

Digital empowerment has given consumers new capabilities, which have not only leveled the playing field, but tipped it in their favor. It used to be that it was only the most important or complex purchases that earned considered attention and effort from potential buyers. Today, since technology has made the due diligence process so much faster and more effortless, consumers apply the same standards of investigation and evaluation to all but the simplest and most inconsequential of products and services. The result is a marketplace in which brands have far fewer controls and are subject to the investigation and judgments of every consumer.

If this sounds like an unforgiving environment, it is. But the good news is that it's now possible for brands to methodically manage and influence this buying process. However, the window for companies to adapt to these new ways of marketing, before the competition moves in first, is closing by the day.

THREATS ABOUND

Sleepy industries are threatened with change on all sides.

Whether your target buyer is B2B or B2C, you are dealing with consumers whose expectations are set by the quality of the experiences they get from the world's most sophisticated and innovative companies, like Amazon, Apple, or Nike. Despite this, many companies, especially those with complex sales, such as in financial services, seem to have avoided all but superficial change. It's almost as if there's been a tacit understanding not to rock the boat too hard among the main players. But if this lock-step hasn't been broken yet in your industry, it probably soon will be. Sleepy industries are threatened with change on all sides.

Suddenly, one company breaks ranks, creates a customer experience that differentiates it from the competition, and everyone is scrambling to catch up. Or it might be start-ups, hunting for industries that are ripe for product innovation and disruption. It might also be the thousand cuts of small entre-preneurs, enabled by technology, and determined to fragment slow-moving targets. And let's not forget the corporate giants, which are also far from idle. They are already way ahead in customer experience, data insights and tech-nology, and they can use their power to steamroll over industry weaknesses when they see opportunity. Amazon, for example, recently announced that it will introduce consumer loans—news that probably made many financial people very nervous.

This book is designed to show company leaders how to turn their busi-nesses into consumer-driven organizations that can successfully respond to, and anticipate, the behaviors and psychology of today's buyers. It lays out a step-by-step plan that will result in a modern, comprehensive marketing sys-tem for today's world. Each chapter is part of a building process, beginning at the foundation and going up; not just considering marketing, but examining every aspect of your organization's relationship with your customers. This is the new model; a customer-centric organization built around the people who keep you in business.

If you're not starting completely from scratch, your organization will probably have in place some of the pieces that we will cover in the coming pages. So, feel free to jump the chapter order and go to the subject that is most important to you. Taken together, however, all seven chapters will show you how to create a complete system that can power your company's growth for years to come.

CHAPTER 1

THINK BEFORE YOU ACT

Develop the strategic plan that shows you what to do and not to do.

EXECUTIVE SUMMARY

- Marketing is too complex today to operate without a plan.
- Your planning should be as comprehensive and evidence-based as possible.
- Your plan should produce a marketing strategy designed to accomplish business goals.
- Your strategy should become a tactical Playbook, for the short and medium-term.
- You should also develop a Roadmap showing how your long-term marketing vision will be accomplished.

TEN STEPS TO A MARKETING PLAN

The following ten steps will result in a comprehensive, actionable marketing plan:

Step 1. Business Goals

Be clear about what business goals marketing has to accomplish, so you can measure performance.

Step 2. Knowledge Gathering

Make sure you know everything about the competition, your consumer, and the marketplace.

Step 3. Gap Analysis

If you don't know something important, find out with original research.

Step 4. Segmentation & Personas

Define your target consumers and zero in on the segments that are most important. Turn them into personas so that you are marketing to people, not numbers.

Step 5. Consumer Journey Mapping

Find out what happens when each key persona takes the journey to purchase and beyond.

Step 6. Channel Strategy

Find out which media channels, from digital to traditional, to use for each persona at different steps in their journey.

Step 7. Messaging Framework

Develop a clear set of messaging parameters for the brand, the personas, channels and contexts.

Step 8. Content Strategy

Develop a comprehensive content strategy that tells you what to say and how to say it to each persona at each interaction point.

Step 9. Tactics

Select tactics that are aligned with the needs identified and that are most likely to accomplish business goals.

Step 10. Playbook & Roadmap

Translate tactics into a 12–24-month Playbook, which acts as the execution guide; also produce a Roadmap laying out the long-term course for your brand.

TACKLING COMPLEXITY

Marketing from your gut today is like trying to hit a target in a blacked-out room. If you hit anything, it's probably by accident.

The new marketing landscape, just like the consumers who inhabit it, is much more complex than it used to be. Instead of just the four big outlets of the past (TV, radio, print, and billboards), today you can add the whole digital world. You also have demanding, digitally savvy consumers with very high expectations, and an unforgiving power to punish brands that manipulate, deceive, or just fail to please.

This requires that companies move in a very thoughtful, careful way, based on data and evidence versus solely their experience or intuition, which is probably already out of date or wrong. Marketing from your gut today is like trying to hit a target in a blacked-out room. If you hit anything it's probably by accident. And for those whose cry is that creativity is the answer, the question is: What happens when the world's best creativity is pointed in the wrong direction?

NOT ROCKET SCIENCE...BUT CLOSE

Marketing strategy tells you what trees need to be in the forest and what it's going to look like in the end.

The strategic marketing planning process that we are going to outline in this first chapter will cover the areas you will need in order to build a marketing system that can manage the new consumer and their needs. You may already be familiar with some of the elements, and some others may even seem to be common sense. Each element is a piece of the puzzle that will inform and guide the design and operation of the marketing system you will need.

The planning process that follows assumes that you already have a business strategy. This should outline the products you'll produce, where your demand will come from, your pricing and the projected return for the business. It includes determining your optimum product- or service-offering mix, distribution strategy, and pricing strategy. Building on that foundation, your marketing mission is to get consumers to buy your products and keep buying them. That's no different to the way it's always been, but the challenges of the complex modern marketplace and consumer are new. That's why a modern marketing system must be informed, precise and on target. It's not rocket science, but there's much more science to it than there used to be.

OWN DON'T RENT

The opportunity is to invest more on Owned and Earned media and save on costly Paid media.

In the old marketing model, most of your company's marketing dollars went to pay third-party media, like magazines or TV, to deliver your message to consumers. You were essentially just renting their communications channel, 30 seconds of time, or a page in this month's magazine. It was the only way (except for perhaps direct mail or outdoor) for a brand to get their story to a lot of prospects.

Today, digital channels are direct to consumer, which allows a company to connect one-to-one and have a two-way conversation with their prospects and consumers. This sets up the potential for creating a new formula that relies less on renting third-party vehicles and more on owning your own communications infrastructure. In the marketing world, we call this *Owned media*. It includes things like your website, mobile sites and email, all of which you own and can do with as you wish. *Paid media*, like TV advertising or banner ads, still has a role in the new marketing, but its responsibility is less than it used to be. Instead of doing all the work of connecting, cultivating and converting, *Paid media* has instead become just one of many triggers that can get the ball rolling.

The third category of media is *Earned media*. Its denotes word-of-mouth exposure that a brand earns from consumers, customers and press. This includes digital versions of word-of-mouth, such as social media, commentary, plus ratings and reviews, as well as traditional earned media, such as PR and press placements. All three types of media are necessary parts of the mix today, but the opportunity is to invest more on *Owned* and *Earned media* and save on costly *Paid media*.

NO EASY SHORTCUTS

You need the same quality of planning for your marketing that you would demand if you were making any other kind of large investment.

Marketing strategy tells you what trees need to be in the forest and what it's going to look like in the end. It shows you how to construct your marketing system so that each piece supports the others and the whole is greater than the sum of its parts. Of course, you need a website, but what do your consumers need it to do? What content should it have and what functionality? And how should it work with your social media websites or your email? Your marketing plan also tells you what to say, when, and in what channels. It tells you how to grow share-of-wallet, where to find more prospects, and even what new products to develop. All of this comes from a methodical strategic process, which delivers a detailed marketing plan.

Unfortunately, many companies confuse strategy and tactics. This is a fundamental mistake that usually comes from the pressure of the moment, "We don't have time; we have to do something!" or being enthralled by the latest fad. Strategy, however, is simply a plan to achieve your business goals. It should show you what tactics to use, when to use them, and how they should work together, synergistically, to accomplish your goals. There's no shortcut to creating a solid plan. It has to be based on evidence, and you need the same quality of planning for your marketing that you would demand if you were making any other kind of large investment.

PEOPLE RULE

Your customer is the center of your world.

The approach that's outlined in this book recognizes the central importance of the consumer in the new business equation, which is why many of the planning activities are organized around understanding the consumer's behavior and attitudes. Your plan will answer five questions:

1. **Who** are our best prospects?
2. **Where** are the right media channels to connect?
3. **When** are the right moments to connect?
4. **What** should we say at every interaction?
5. **How** should we say it?

STEP 1. BUSINESS GOALS

KNOW WHAT THEY ARE

Marketing is the new field of battle where winners and losers are decided.

Few senior business leaders, especially of smaller companies, *want* to do marketing. It's often perceived as a cost that reduces their potential profitability, and for many feels pretty squishy. In fairness, before the digital age, it *was* pretty squishy. The famous quip from John Wanamaker sums it up: "Half the money I spend on advertising is wasted; the trouble is I don't know which half." But that day has gone, thank goodness, and marketing is now about as measurable and accountable as most other business activities.

Today, the reality is that any company that wants to win and keep customers must invest in marketing. That's because marketing is the new field of battle where winners and losers are decided. While things like supply chain management used to determine success or failure, today they are table stakes in the competitive game of acquiring and retaining customers.

It is the business of marketing to ensure that strategies and tactics align to business goals.

Marketing, thanks to technology, is now a measurable investment and is subject to the same accountability of all business investments. That means having specified goals, key performance indicators and measurable ROI. Objectives can be growing share, revenue, entering new markets, introducing new products, or whatever is strategically important to the company as long as it aligns with the greater business goals. Setting business goals, however, is not the job of marketing except to the degree that the planning work marketing does can help reveal business opportunities or challenges. But it is the business of marketing to ensure that their strategies and tactics align to business goals.

After watching the growth of Tesla and the evolution of Google and Apple in the car space, Toyota began to transition its business goals to include self-driving cars. This shift in goals led to a complex balancing act for their marketing because of the need to integrate customer expectations of enjoying driving with the new idea of having the car drive for you. As a result, Toyota's business strategy has shifted to a two-pronged approach with the long-term goal of fully autonomous cars and the near-term development of semi-autonomous technology. This will now have to translate to the way the company talks to consumers at every interaction.

Whatever your company's business goals, you need to make sure it is clear what marketing can and should do to help achieve them. Goals should be detailed, time-specific, and measurable enough so that you can evaluate the ability of strategies and tactics to achieve them.

STEP 2. KNOWLEDGE GATHERING

FILLING IN THE PICTURE

The more you know, the better your plan will be.

You need to know everything relevant about your customers, prospects, the competition, the category, what's worked and what's not worked. This begins by exploring the knowledge that exists within your company. First, gather any research that has been conducted. Even old research is better than none. Add to this any public research that is available and consider buying any current research studies about your category or target audience. Many industries have A&U (attitude and usage) studies available, which explore consumer behavior and attitudes in specific industries and product categories.

Extract the knowledge that exists within your own teams but which may not be generally shared within the organization.

Next, conduct internal stakeholder interviews to help fill in the picture. This is very important because it allows you to extract the knowledge that exists within your own teams, but which may not be generally shared within the organization. This should be mostly focused on the consumer, with attention to the customer experience, the sales process, attitudes, and the post-sale relationship. Much of this is anecdotal, but it can be very valuable. The easiest way to do this is to talk to senior executives and practice leaders. They will have deeply experienced perspectives about barriers and opportunities. Also, continue the data-gathering part of the process with a distillation of any metrics you currently have. This includes sales trend data, sales data by product type and geographical area, and any other key factors that may be important for your industry. It should also include marketing data such as metrics for your website, mobile sites, email open and view rates, search performance, CRM, and loyalty participation and performance.

Throughout this initial set of activities, you should begin to be on the lookout for clues that will lead you to consumer insights. These are the "aha" moments, which give you an insight that your competition may not have stumbled upon yet. Studying the market led Bill Gates to think that computer manufacturers would prefer to buy an operating system, rather than make their own. That's why he bought an existing operating system from a small Seattle company, developed it into MS-DOS and licensed it to IBM for PCs. Much as Gates had divined, PC cloners such as Compaq decided it was cheaper to use the IBM operating system instead of making their own. Within two years, Microsoft sales exploded.

SIZING UP YOUR RIVALS

If you don't know what the competition is doing, it can blindside you.

Next, conduct a competitive evaluation. Make sure you have a comprehensive understanding not only of the strengths and weaknesses of your competitors' offerings, but also how they go to market. This includes how they differentiate themselves, what marketing channels they are in, what audiences they are targeting, how much they spend, and what messaging they use and have used in the past. You will also need to know what their visual or creative approach is, the strengths and weaknesses of their customer experience (CX) in all channels, their mobile strategy, and, if relevant, how they present themselves at retail.

TAPPING INTO SENTIMENT

Social Listening and Search Term research are invaluable.

Regardless of time or budget restrictions, be sure to take advantage of the considerable insights you can get from *Social Listening research* and *Search Term research*. The former will give you a glimpse into what people are talking about online in social channels. The latter will tell you what people are interested in when they search as well as the words and phrases they use related to your category. Both are usually very enlightening; but like most research, they only provide a piece of the picture. When combined with other inputs and insights, they will help to point you in the right direction.

It could be the freshest, most up-to-the-minute research you will have.

Social listening, or social media monitoring as it is sometimes called, is a customer intelligence tool that tells you what people are saying in public social media channels. While it cannot give you insights into all social conversations, you can see what people are saying in blogs, reviews, comment sections, and social networks, such as Twitter. You can search for company names, both your own and the competition's, or you can search for words associated with your product category. You can also examine different timeframes and even specific locations. For example, you could search for posts that mention auto insurance in the first quarter in Los Angeles. Either way, social listening provides a wonderfully rich and comparatively inexpensive way to see inside your consumer's head on a regular and timely basis. Tapping into consumer sentiment is an important part of the strategic process at the outset, and it should also be part of the ongoing health check of your brand.

Similarly, Search Term research gives you a window into what search terms people use. Search has become the almost inevitable first step in every consumer's journey to buy almost everything. We take it for granted that it can, and will, deliver the answer to every question, the facts about every product, and guidance on every subject. The truth, however, is far short of this expectation, which is an opportunity for brands that we will discuss later. Search Term research can, however, tell you not only what search terms to buy with SEM (search engine marketing like Google AdWords), but also what content has the greatest likelihood of being picked up by the search engines for inclusion in organic or natural search results. Like Social Listening, there are many tools available to help mine the gold hidden in consumer search activity. Both areas have become well developed with many options that are easily accessible.

STEP 3. GAP ANALYSIS

KNOW WHAT YOU DON'T KNOW

Make sure you are confident there are no surprises lurking.

With all this information in hand, you next need to figure out what you know and what you don't know. These are obviously judgments, but someone has to determine if the knowledge you have collected is sufficient and reliable, and to see if any gaps exist. The danger, of course, is in not knowing what you don't know, and marching on blindly assuming all is well. A Bain & Company survey of 362 firms found that 80% of companies believed they had a superior customer experience. But their customers said that only 8% of them were really delivering. If they had checked their assumptions with their customers, they would have known this.

As with most things in life, mistakes and omissions made early are often amplified later on.

That's why it's common sense to make sure your conclusions are based on inputs that are as fresh, complete and as reliable as is practicably possible. This is even more important considering how fast the market, the competition and consumers change today. Sony, for example, was focused on a brick-and-mortar strategy for stores, but because they only stocked 70% of their catalogue in the stores, they had a gap in their offering and more importantly, their customer experience. Fresh research showed that the integration of stores and the internet would not only close the gap, but also serve growing consumer expectations to experience products in a store first and then buy them online, called "showrooming." Without research, they wouldn't have known this until customers started to complain, by which time damage would have already been done. Since there is usually not enough time and money to do everything perfectly, close as many gaps as you can under your circumstances.

SURVEY SAYS...

If you hit a big question mark, you have to stop and find out the answers.

The synthesis of all the knowledge you have gathered will form a picture of your consumer, your brand's perception, your category and your competition. Some unanswered questions, such as what your consumer's social responsibility priorities are, you might feel comfortable bypassing. Whereas other questions, such as what your audience values in terms of benefits, will need to be answered before you make marketing decisions. Of course, it's always painful to stop the momentum toward actually getting things done, but if you hit a big question mark, you have to stop and find out the answers with fresh research.

Even a small piece of original research with your customers or your prospects is better than nothing at all.

Research doesn't have to break the bank. Solutions run from online panels to focus groups. There are hundreds of research options, both quantitative and qualitative. Different questions require different approaches:
- Who is my audience? (quantitative)
- How do they make purchase decisions? (quantitative)
- How do they feel about specific brands/trends? (qualitative)
- What problems do they have in getting what they need? (qual+quant)
- What are they thinking, feeling when they are shopping? (qualitative)

STEP 4. SEGMENTATION & PERSONAS

SHARPEN YOUR FOCUS

The most important job of segmentation is in guiding you to the consumer segments that have the most potential.

Like most companies, you probably have a solid idea of the makeup of your target audience, but for the purposes of marketing, we need to have a very clear picture of the composition of that universe. You need to understand the relative importance of one segment versus another, which to prioritize and why.

These groups might be divided by age, or behavior, or some other characteristics. The essential thing is that the reason for the segment should be important to the brand and a defining characteristic of the group. Segmentation is critical because most companies have more than one target audience, and each usually behaves very differently from the others.

The most important job of segmentation is in guiding you to the consumer segments that have the most potential for your company. Segmentation also lays the groundwork for the kind of data profiling that will only become more prevalent as data technologies become more accessible to companies of all sizes. It sets up a company's ability to make educated guesses at probable behavior. So, for example, if people in a segment tend to work out regularly, you might infer that everyone with that same behavior profile is likely to be into fitness. Famously, Target inferred that a teenage girl was pregnant based on her buying behavior. When her father complained that the company was encouraging his high school daughter to get pregnant with coupons for baby clothes, a manager apologized profusely. A few days later when another manager called to again say sorry, it was the father's turn to apologize. He explained he had spoken with his daughter, and she had admitted that she was, after all, pregnant.

The process of conducting a segmentation study should actually show where clusters of similarity exist and in doing so may reveal hidden opportunities.

Segmentation can be by geography, demographics, behavior, lifestyle, frequency of use and much more. The process of conducting a segmentation study should actually show where clusters of similarity exist and in doing so may reveal hidden opportunities. This work should be research based versus informed guessing. Industry-focused studies are available for purchase, but they are often too broad for the specific needs of one product or service category, which may lead you to original research.

Coming out of a segmentation study, a company should be able to identify which discrete segments it makes sense to pursue. Clearly many considerations factor into these decisions such as the size of the market, growth potential, value, maturity, competition, etc. Much of the other research you have gathered (and your business goals) will help, but a judgment is called for before we go on to the next step of creating personas. The idea is to get focused with a manageable number of segments, often three to five. Too many will spread your efforts, and budget, too thinly and may create operational problems down the road.

This may be the first situation in this process where you encounter the challenges of choice. Many people in companies, when faced with choices, defer to avoidance; if you pick everything then you can't be wrong. But the resulting lack of focus, which starts early with things such as the number of segments you choose to concentrate on, can be extremely debilitating and can often be an augur of dysfunctionality to come. This is an institutional culture problem and, while not the subject of this book, one of the bigger barriers to positive change in most companies.

FLESH & BLOOD PEOPLE

Forrester studies indicate that planning with personas can actually improve the effectiveness of critical initiatives by as much as 400%.

While segmentation is important and valuable, a sheet of numbers is not enough for a customer-oriented organization, which is what you need to be. Therefore, to bring the reality of your target audience to life and keep it alive, not only for your marketing teams, but also for every person in the company, you need to create personas.

It's too easy to forget that your prospects and customers are Flesh-and-Blood People and not numbers to be counted.

Personas are simply profiles of the typical person in a segment. The idea is to help you and your teams internalize the emotional reality of the target consumer you are marketing to and relate to them as human beings. Sure, there may come a time when your marketing bots are selling to their buying bots, but we are still quite far off from that. If you are selling to people, your brand experiences will always have to be this mushy mix of analytical and emotional elements, just like people. Personas help you get, and keep, the mix right. Be sure to define your personas by age, gender, location, education and family, as well as by goals, challenges, values, and fears. To cap it off, it's also helpful to have a visual of the persona and an encapsulated pitch that would resonate with them. Each target persona will help guide your team through the subsequent steps in the planning and execution process.

Once you have target personas, spread them widely through your organization, and bring your customers to life for your teams in any creative way you can. Some companies create persona rooms, or spaces designed to reflect the life and preferences of a persona. Staff can go there to immerse themselves in the images and emotional icons of a particular persona and hope for empathy and inspiration. Personas work.

STEP 5. CONSUMER JOURNEY MAPPING

WALKING IN THEIR SHOES

Customer experience is the field of competitive battle for the foreseeable future.

We are all familiar with the sales funnel, but it's worth another brief look. At the top, it shows how a brand captures a wide swath of prospects, which through attrition during the marketing and sales process, is winnowed down to a much smaller number of buyers at the bottom. This is still essentially what happens. We set a wide net and yet only end up with a small fraction of prospects as buyers. The funnel is useful as a measure of the quantity of leads at each narrowing point in a sales process. But it doesn't show us how to influence the thinking, and by extension, the number of consumers through the stages of the funnel.

A great concept for this is the *Consumer Decision Journey*. First devised by McKinsey & Co. in 2009, this is a representation of the consumer's journey from initial awareness all the way through purchase and then on to loyalty and advocacy. It's a valuable conceptual model that helps us focus on creating better experiences at each interaction point. It teaches us how to influence behaviors that lead to conversion, repeat purchase, loyalty, and advocacy.

Unlike the funnel, it recognizes the importance of the loyalty part of the journey: a reflection of how powerful the post-sale influence of every consumer has become. The result is not a funnel, but a loop, where the initial purchase is just a stop along the road.

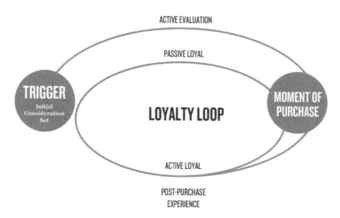

The objective of journey mapping is to chart the journeys that different personas take from initial awareness to first purchase and then through the experience of being a customer. This tells you what their steps and interactions are likely to be. It also reveals the primary influences that shape attitudes and preferences along the way. If your mission is to truly serve the consumer and to anticipate their needs and wants, journey mapping becomes a central tool.

According to the Association of National Advertisers, journey mapping translates to better business performance, with top performing companies having a better grasp of their customer journey than low performers.

Not surprisingly, Amazon is really good at this. Their customer experience mapping focuses on how personalization and recommendations can humanize, as well as simplify and smooth, the consumer experience. At the same time, they have a deep understanding of how buyers discover, research, and evaluate purchase decisions. This leads to Amazon appearing consistently in search results, providing content, access, and information to assist buyers and entice them into their orbit.

TEASING OUT THE INSIGHTS

The average shopper uses multiple sources of information to make a decision.

As we've discussed, each persona is different, and, as such, has a unique journey that requires its own mapping. The mapping exercise can take two forms. The first is a workshop with key company stakeholders; the second is an exploration directly with target consumer segments. Obviously, it's best to do both kinds of exploration; however, when pressed for time and budget, the internal stakeholder route should be the minimum.

The stakeholder workshop is designed to tease out the knowledge of the customer journey that exists within your organization. It should be made up of key leaders as well as people who deal with customers on a day-to-day basis, such as sales and customer service. Participants share their knowledge of what happens on consumer journeys. It makes for great discussions and valuable insights. It also makes these key internal stakeholders more likely to actively use your journey maps to guide their ongoing customer-experience efforts.

Journey maps can help companies see themselves as their customers do.

In every case, you want to understand what's happening at each of the key stages in the consumer decision journey. These stages can be generally described as:

Consumer Journey:

1. **Trigger**—What causes a consumer to begin thinking about a purchase?
2. **Consideration**—Is this purchase necessary and feasible? What will it mean?
3. **Evaluation**—Which product is better and why?
4. **Purchase**—How and where is the purchase completed? Is it easy?
5. **Loyalty**—What is the experience of the product? Will customers become advocates?

Different industries or product categories may have different stages. But whatever they are, at each of these key stages in the journey you want to figure out the consumer's goals and emotions: the triggers, pain points and service gaps. You want to know the media channels they use and what they're doing when they use them, what content is needed at each stage, what kind of experience they want, what tools might be useful, what the brand's role should be, and how you will measure performance. You also need to identify those interactions that are true *Moments of Truth*, as McKinsey called them, which define or change a consumer's perception of the brand.

Together, these inputs start to build a comprehensive picture of how each persona navigates their journey. At our office, we map these journeys on a giant corkboard so that we can see the journey as a whole. It helps us to keep the big picture in mind as we search for those magic insights that can become the basis for competitive differentiation. These insights might tell us where consumers need more help or information, what needs, or attributes are being missed, or what might make their journey easier and more enjoyable.

With these maps in hand you are a step closer to understanding where to focus your marketing efforts; what channels and even media vehicles to use; what ideas, words and phrases the consumer responds to at each interaction; and most importantly, which steps along the journey are the most effective for creating brand preference.

STEP 6. CHANNEL STRATEGY

THE PERFECT MIX

Managing channel mix will be table stakes in the competitive arena.

By this stage, you have a good idea of your target personas and their consumer decision journeys. You now need to start to make some decisions, the first of which is to identify the key moments of engagement. This is the beginning of a practical plan that tells you *when* you need to engage.

You will also need to know *where* to engage. For example, if your product is auto parts and your target persona is an auto enthusiast, you might have identified websites like CarDomain, or MotorAuthority for the Trigger stage. This then goes into your Channel Strategy, which enables you to focus your resources on the channels that you think will have the greatest impact on a particular target segment at each stage of the journey. As most mapping exercises reveal, at each stage there are many channels and influences, so part of the process is to winnow them down to those that give you the greatest impact. This recognizes that you cannot and should not try to do everything. As Clausewitz said, "To achieve victory we must mass our forces at the hub of all power and movement." Your mission is to break into awareness, and concentrating your forces gives you a better chance of getting through the consumer's mental defenses.

A Channel Strategy creates a plan for where a company should focus its time and money at each different stage of the journey.

Channels include everything from retail and customer service to traditional media, digital channels, mobile and social sites. It's a loose classification, like many marketing terms, and can mean a type of channel, like mobile, or a specific channel, like Facebook. Each channel has its own rules, requirements, unique consumer dynamics and levels of investment. All of these should factor into the decision making because channels should not be entered into lightly. All too often brands put a toe in the water, such as with Facebook or, frequently, mobile apps, and find that they really didn't understand what was required to succeed. Walmart initially failed to understand social dynamics when it treated social media as an advertising channel. This can be because brands simply don't do their homework, or just because they're jumping onto a trendy bandwagon without thinking it through.

THE LAYER EFFECT

Integrated marketing is impossible without adapting channel mix to the customer journey.

Different channels are better suited to different tasks at different times. Channels that might work for creating awareness might not be right for cultivating preference. That's why a Channel Strategy creates a plan for *where* a company should focus its time and money at each different stage of the journey. People hurrying to their plane on an airport concourse might see an ad that triggers awareness and even the intention of going to a website to find out more, but it can't be expected to make the pitch, because the time and place aren't right. In the marketing world, we call that *context* and it's a critical consideration in evaluating channels. Another important consideration is how channels layer on top of one another creating a cumulative effect.

Recognizing that no one channel tactic stands in isolation, marketers need to carefully consider the cumulative effects of tactics over time.

Messaging and impressions created in one channel are layered on top of those created in other channels and the result may not be simply additive. This should not only take into account message and brand consistency, but also how one channel hands off to another, and the way a brand's value proposition is best presented.

Channel strategy can, and should over time, be expanded to include a plan for how to optimize channels based on performance. The process of watching performance metrics, as marketing plans are executed, reveals which channels are working, which are not, and where opportunities to refocus on winning channels may exist. It may also identify channels that are more effective with different personas, products, or offers. Channel strategy is, therefore, a living, marketing operations tool, as well as a planning tool.

STEP 7. MESSAGING FRAMEWORK

THE MAGIC WORDS

Messaging frameworks show you how to be more persuasive.

The mission is to create a system that puts content in front of a consumer at just the right moment. But all your work stands or falls on what happens then, and success is no accident. It's the result of delivering content that communicates exactly the right message for that particular consumer at that moment in time. Helping to set the stage for this is your *Messaging Framework*.

Messaging Frameworks are used to understand how to be more persuasive. Just like good salespeople learn the most effective pitch and practice it for that critical time with a prospect, so too do organizations have to study their audiences to know exactly what to say to get them to take the desired action. The Centers for Disease Control and Prevention (CDC), for example, studied African-American women's social interactions and influences in order to figure out how to persuade them to get early mammograms. The CDC used the *Persuasive Health Message Framework* to communicate more effectively with their target audience. As a result, screening in the implementation areas is now 46% higher.

Organizations have to study their audiences to know exactly what to say, to get them to take the desired action.

A Messaging Framework brings together the four messaging components that should shape your content. It's a guide for your creative and marketing teams as they turn your strategies into tactics. Some of the framework you may have already, some may be understood, but not well articulated, and you may still have some work left to do.

Messaging Framework:

1. **Brand Messaging**—Brand promise, positioning, mission, tagline, and overall voice & tone.
2. **Value Proposition**—Product sales pillars, the big idea and evidence that supports claims
3. **Persona Messaging**—Approach for each specific target segment.
4. **Tactical Modifiers**—How context or channel modify a message.

A solid Messaging Framework reflects how well you know your brand, your consumers and your competitive marketplace. All messages, regardless of channel or persona, should ladder back to it. It's the underpinnings of your *Content Strategy* and can make the difference between content that resonates and content that lands with a thud.

STEP 8. CONTENT STRATEGY

MAKE IT ENGAGING

Consumers prefer to learn from content rather than ads.

If you think about your own buying behavior for a moment, you will quickly recognize that advertising has less influence on you than it used to. For most people, advertising still creates awareness and gives you general impressions about brands, but you don't probably rely on it for the information you need to make buying decisions. Instead, you know that within seconds you can identify the major brands within a category, visit their websites, read reviews and ratings, see social posts, watch informative videos and generally be immersed in knowledge on virtually any subject. Consumers, like you, have an expectation that with search and the internet at their fingertips they can make the best, smartest, most fully informed decisions every time. The reality, however, is different.

> There is almost too much information; it's disorganized.
> A lot of it is misleading or deceptive, and most of us don't
> want to put that much effort into the entire process.
> This is an opportunity for brands.

Decades ago when Bill Gates said, "Content is king," he may have been underestimating things. Today, content is the fuel that powers the modern marketing engine. While consumers theoretically just want all the data and information, they actually want it neatly packaged and wrapped with an engaging little bow. In other words, consumers want someone else to do all the work for them. They want someone to bring them what they need to know, to tell them what's important to consider and what's not, to make sure it is useful and accurate, and to make the whole process and experience, fast, easy, and engaging. Regardless of what business you are in, you can be sure that your buyers prefer you to do their work for them. And if consumers come to believe that you will reliably deliver credible, valuable content in the form they want, when they want it, you will quickly get on their short list. Not too many brands make that list. It's a mental list of companies and brands in each category that consumers can trust, not unlike the positioning ladder that Reis & Trout identified in 1980.

A TOUGH CROWD

> People think most brand content is disappointing.

Content can be an article on a blog, an interactive tool on your website, an eBook, a white paper, a video, a podcast, or a touch screen at an airport. Content is everywhere in a thousand forms, and it seems like every company that's ever read an article on content marketing is producing it. Most of it, however, is not very good, which is why it's so important to get right. As a Pardot survey revealed, 71% of respondents reported being disappointed with a brand's content, and 64% indicated that they would not be very likely to ever engage with a brand again that had made a poor first impression.

What makes content good is not just good creativity, but saying exactly the right thing to a consumer for that moment in time.

The right content says the right thing, to the right person at the right time, in the right place, in the right way. Getting all these things right might seem like threading a very small needle, but it's what you, or any other demanding consumer, expects. It's a standard set by the very sophisticated brand experiences that consumers have become accustomed to. Zappos, known for its legendary customer service, also recognizes the importance of having a strong content strategy. Pinterest is a prime channel for their content, which is tightly themed and targeted to their key segments, such as brides-to-be. Their 30-plus Pinterest boards range from *"Here comes the bride"* to *"Stuff I wish my boyfriend wears."* Each is narrowly targeted to feed the psychology of someone with a specific interest at a particular moment.

Informed by your Messaging Framework and Consumer Journey Maps, you can plan the most effective content approaches for each persona at each of the key engagement points you've identified. Everything you have learned about your target audiences, what they do, how they feel, and what they are looking for, will contribute as you distill all the knowledge and insights you've gained into your Content Strategy. This will then inform and direct everything your teams do from this point on.

STEP 9. TACTICS

PICKING WINNERS

The right tactics reveal themselves through the process.

While most of us understand the difference between strategy and tactics, in the heat of battle the two can get confused. Jeremiah Owyang of the webstrategist.com, sums up the classic way to think about it: "Strategy is done above the shoulders, tactics are done below the shoulders." While that's true, executing tactics today requires smart, adaptive, on-the-ground thinking by everyone involved.

Your Marketing Plan so far:

1. *Consumer Segments* and *Personas*, so you know **WHO** you're going after.
2. *Consumer Decision Journey* maps telling you **WHEN** to engage each segment.
3. *Channel Strategies* telling you **WHERE** to connect with each segment.
4. *Messaging Framework* articulating **WHAT** to say at each interaction.
5. *Content Strategy* showing **HOW** to say it most effectively.
6. *Tactics* that potentially align with the above.

A tactic not based on a strategy is an accident waiting to happen.

With defined business goals and clear strategies in hand, the next step is to pick your tactics.

This is the time to resist the siren song of the latest fad. The problem is that most of the marketing stories you and your colleagues read about today are tactics, not strategies. It might be a social network like Snapchat or Periscope, some innovative software platform, a hot TV show, or just what your competition is doing. Whatever everyone is talking about is probably a tactic, not a strategy. And, a tactic not based on a strategy is an accident waiting to happen. When a client of ours prioritized investing in Second Life over their website, just because **IBM** was doing it, we knew we were in the power of a fad. Hopefully you can resist these pressures and make the smart choices you need with a clear-eyed, analytical process. It will ensure that you prioritize tactics with the highest potential to achieve the business results you need.

Evaluate Tactics:

1. Suitability for a particular touch-point and segment
2. How it will be measured
3. Performance projections based in evidence
4. Estimated costs to implement
5. Internal and external staffing requirements
6. Other required resources

Tactics fall into one of the three media buckets: *Owned, Earned,* or *Paid.* A tactic could be an ad campaign, which runs and then is no more, or a mobile app that will live for a couple of years. Some will be easy to implement, and others will require that you have pieces of marketing infrastructure in place with specific capabilities, such as a website with ratings and reviews. Prioritizing tactics will draw on all these considerations, budget realities, time frame and business goals. It's a balancing act, not only considering all the costs, timing and difficulty of execution, but also the less quantifiable qualities, such as uniqueness and remarkability. This is one of the areas where it takes the discipline of a scientist combined with the vision of an artist to make brilliant decisions. It's also why Artificial Intelligence will not be replacing our jobs any time soon.

STEP 10. PLAYBOOK & ROADMAP

EXECUTING WELL

A good idea without good execution will go nowhere.

Congratulations, you have now reached the final step in your marketing planning process. You already have most of the answers you need. You've clarified your business goals, sifted through your internal knowledge, gathered whatever else is out there, filled the gaps with research, reviewed the competition, studied your consumers, articulated your strategy, and selected the best tactics. Along the way you've discovered consumer insights that will help set your brand apart, you've learned how to improve your customer experience, and you've uncovered product and service opportunities. All of this is for naught, however, if you don't execute well.

As Jim Collins confirmed in *Good to Great*, you don't get success without the ability to execute well. But anybody running a business already knows that and struggles with it every day; it's no different for marketing.

All the great planning in the world will not amount to much if it isn't translated into action. That's why the final output of your planning process is not a strategy document, but a playbook.

THE YELLOW BRICK ROAD

Most executives don't think their company is good at execution.

The Playbook provides the step-by-step game plan for executing your medium-term marketing strategy. It's the execution guide that everyone involved should follow. It prioritizes tactics, provides an outline of each, a timeline, estimated cost, how they will be measured, projected performance, internal responsibilities, company resources required, and what's needed from agencies or other vendors.

It's the yellow brick road they follow to get your short and medium-term marketing objectives accomplished. It's not only how you keep everyone on the same page, but an important driver in the general effort to shift company culture to a consumer focus.

The Playbook is designed to be shared with all involved and key stakeholders, so everyone knows what's going to happen, when and why.

Most Playbooks should look at no more than a one-to-two-year period. With consumer behavior, technology, and the competition changing so rapidly, it's essential to be able to react and adapt very quickly. That's why revisiting the inputs to your strategic planning at least once a year is important, if you want to avoid nasty surprises.

The Playbook also incorporates a summary of your strategy, including your personas, to remind everyone involved in execution what the mission is and who you are targeting. Teams use it to guide their tactical efforts and cross-reference it with the findings from the Content Strategy.

As we will see in Chapter 7, in order for you to create a marketing system, you have to put pieces of technology and content infrastructure in place. This may take more time than you have before you need to see results. So the final piece of your planning output should be a Roadmap that charts a course for the long term.

KEEPING THE END IN MIND

The Roadmap paints the picture of your ideal marketing system and prioritizes the steps to get there.

Your Roadmap has a longer time horizon than your Playbook. It lays out the step-by-step process of putting in place the pieces of your marketing system over the long term. Like Rome, a sophisticated marketing system is not built in a day. It includes all the technology and content infrastructure you will need, as well as things like developing a consumer database and achieving brand preference, which doesn't happen overnight. While you might want a loyalty program, it might not make sense until you've put your CRM system in place and built out your full line of products to enable cross-selling. Like any good city planner, you start with a vision of how you want the city to look and work when it's finished. Then you prioritize the steps it's going to take to get there. The Roadmap is important because your immediate marketing plan will not reflect the total vision for everything marketing can and should do. Your Roadmap describes that vision and keeps you on course over the long haul.

With your Playbook and Roadmap completed, you have articulated a long-term marketing vision and a medium-term action plan. These are based on the evidence you have gathered. Those inputs will be good for a while, but it's smart to check them at least every year or more frequently. This means going through the ten steps outlined above to see if any of your assumptions or inputs might be based on out-of-date information, to see if consumer behavior has changed, or if the competition has evolved in a significant way.

A regular formal review and health check of your marketing plan is essential in a fast-changing world.

The Playbook is also a very good budgeting tool. It already has buy-in from many levels and areas of your organization, and it breaks down what you are going to spend and when you are going to spend it. The associated Roadmap also outlines what infrastructure you will need to support the Playbook and estimated costs. This might be a new website, for example. Much of this infrastructure is usually classified as a capital expense, which can relieve some pressure on your marketing budget.

CHAPTER 2

THE ENGINE FOR GROWTH

Ensure you have a healthy brand ready to go to market

EXECUTIVE SUMMARY

- Your brand is your most important asset—this is even more true in the digital age where advertising has become less effective.
- Your brand is the guiding principle for your company—brands only succeed when they deliver on their promises, and that takes the entire organization.
- Creating and bringing a brand to life builds more lasting equity— a strong brand will create more value than advertising, and for less investment.
- Strong brands don't happen by accident—invest the time and effort to create your brand methodically.

STEPS TO A STRONG BRAND

Branding is complex, but nothing is more important to get right. If a company doesn't create its own brand, its customers and competition will do it for them.

1. **Create your Brand Promise**
   - Your *Brand Promise* is the promise you make to consumers and it rests on the foundation of your *Brand Purpose*, which is not making money, but doing something for the greater good.
   - From this flows your *Brand Mission*, which is what your product is specifically trying to accomplish.

- These are both kept alive every day by your organization living your *Brand Values.*
- Your *Brand Promise* sits on this unchanging foundation and is made up of your *Value Proposition* and *Brand Positioning* versus your competition.
- In a world of empowered, socially connected consumers, a brand must deliver on its promise consistently, everywhere.

2. **Choose your Brand Personality**
   - Your *Brand Personality* is the unique character of your brand. It is what emotionally sets your brand apart.
   - It is expressed visually and through the voice and tone you display in all the creative expressions of your brand.

3. **Define your Brand Identity**
   - *Brand Identity* brings together all the facets of the brand into an integrated concept.
   - At the center is the *Brand Essence*, which becomes the rallying cry for your employees as they bring your brand to life.
   - This is supported by the *Brand Pillars*, key brand directives, which keep employees focused on what's important.

1. THE VALUE OF A BRAND

THE ENGINE FOR GROWTH

The trust that a brand can earn often tips the balance.

You would be surprised how often otherwise sophisticated business leaders say things like, "I don't have time for branding, I need results now!" Of course, these same people never have time for branding, which is one reason why the results they seek are always so elusive.

This chapter will discuss why you need a brand, how to make one, and the value it brings. It's an especially important underpinning to the "considered purchase" process that new consumers go through as they decide which brands to trust. Despite the intention of modern consumers to be analytical and methodical about picking brands, the trust that a brand can earn often tips the balance.

Without brands, we would all quickly be reduced to selling product benefits and price, and before long everything would be commoditized, and margins would disappear. Branding adds the value of an emotional, human dimension, creating relationships with consumers that go beyond the analytical. It offers companies the opportunity to elevate the perception of their strengths and can even protect against their weaknesses. The strength of a brand saves companies when they fail, such as with the VW fiasco, and amplifies their victories when they succeed, such as with the Tesla 3 introduction. Unlike an advertising campaign, your brand is not short term but meant to last. It becomes the engine for your growth in share, profit, and markets. Overtime your brand can and should become your company's most valuable asset.

> **The strength of a brand saves companies when they fail and amplifies their victories when they succeed.**

Despite our attempts to be coldly rational and analytical in our purchases, all buyers, B2B and B2C, are always influenced by their emotions. This is important to remember, because it's easy to forget that brands are actually all about people, rather than products. Strangely, it has taken the influence of technology for the human component to rise in importance. Whereas David Ogilvy, in the simpler days of Mad Men, described a brand as "the intangible sum of a product's attributes," Jeff Bezos, founder of Amazon, says: "A brand for a company is like a reputation for a person."

In today's world where distribution is less of a barrier to competition, brands have become a more important differentiator than ever. Despite that, many company leaders often invest little in this comparatively mushy thing called branding. From the perspective that would love to reduce all of business to the predictability of engineering, it is understandable. However, in a marketplace dominated by the emotions of consumers, it's really dangerous, in most instances, to ignore your brand.

THE SHARING SOCIETY

> **Finding out what other people are saying about their brand experiences is easy and fast.**

You probably know that the idea of branding comes from literally putting your mark on your livestock. That basic idea was perfected in Ogilvy's day and grew to include ideas and beliefs but was still somewhat superficial. Since the advent of the digital age, however, brands have come to mean much more. At the root of this evolution is our easy access to information, and the consumer's ability to affect a brand by quickly and widely exchanging opinions. Sharing experiences, or seeing what other people are saying about their brand experiences, is easy and fast. Whereas branding used to be predominantly about what companies say; today it's more about what they actually do. Of course, the way a company behaves has always been important. The difference is that before the internet, if you had a poor experience with a brand, all you could usually do was write them a letter or tell your friends at work. Today, on the other hand, if brands don't perform, consumers can and will punish them in social media, ratings and reviews, and more. For consumers, it's easy and quick; for brands, it's lasting and can be enormously damaging.

> **Branding used to be predominantly about what companies say. Today, it's more about what they actually do.**

Even with Sears on the ropes, Craftsman tools remained "America's most trusted tool brand" until Sears moved manufacturing to China, sacrificing quality and the *Made in America* label, in the process. Then social media posts like this one started lighting up the internet: "For many years my family, Dad, Grandpa, and uncles used Craftsman tools. Won't buy another, ever. Make them in America again!!!" Sears betrayed the fundamental idea of their brand and thought consumers wouldn't notice or say anything. Conversely, if a brand does a good job it can be very valuable, not just for the business at that particular moment, but for the overall strength and value of the brand going forward. IBM strengthens its overall brand with every success of Watson, its super-computer, ranging from new mobile commerce platforms to winning on Jeopardy.

DELIVERING GROWTH

Strong brands do better than weak brands.

A study by WPP's BrandZ between 2004 and 2015 measured the ability of brands to deliver in three key areas: differentiated value proposition, Brand

Identity, and advertising. Brands that did well on all three measures had value growth of 168% over the 10-year period. But brands that were weak in all three areas grew their value by only 21%. This big disparity in financial performance speaks to the value of having a healthy, aligned brand. In 2014, for example, strong brands outperformed the market by 73% according to McKinsey, up from 62% in just 2013, and according to Gallup, which has done many studies on brand value, getting this alignment right actually doubles share-of-wallet.

While some companies have adjusted to the new realities, many still haven't.

Alignment means that the promise a brand makes to its target consumers is not only understood and valued by those consumers, but it is actually delivered at every touch point. It means that the purpose and values of the brand are clear, meaningful and real, and that there is a consistency to the Brand Personality and identity across the board. This can't be just some marketing veneer anymore. It must be the guiding principle of the brand and the organization behind it. That includes all the people who bring the brand to life for consumers every day. Despite this, Gallup tells us that less than half of managers, and only a third of rank-and-file employees, say they know what their company stands for and what makes them different. This underscores the notion that while some companies have adjusted to the new realities, many still haven't. Hopefully, if you are reading this, your company is in the process of making this shift. What your brand needs to be and how it needs to be structured in order to be relevant and compelling to today's consumers will be a huge part of your winning formula.

2. BRAND HEALTH

GET CHECKED

What do consumers really think of your brand?

Before you go to market you need to make sure you have a healthy brand. This means that the way your brand is perceived and articulated by your consumers and employees is not only contributing to the business results you seek, but it is what you intend it to be.

If you are not sure where you stand, there are many ways to determine your status. These include brand health studies, Net Promoter Scores, social listening surveys, as well as looking at your financial performance. In today's world, your brand has become a key driver of your business performance and will be a clear indicator of how healthy your business is. One way or another, considering its importance, it's probably a good idea to review your brand's current condition.

It's probably a good idea to review your brand's current condition.

First, you need to look at the key components that make up a meaningful, compelling brand today. That means going through a methodical, thoughtful process.

NEW SCHOOL

We have entered a "trust but verify" world.

Brands are symbols, shorthand for all of a consumer's feelings and experiences—an easier way to navigate a world full of thousands of companies and products. Your logo, tag line, style guide and other visual elements are expressions of your brand, but they are not your brand. A brand is the sum of all the ideas that define a product or company's place in the world. Old school, brute force marketing had brands trying to shout louder than their competitors, pushing features and benefits, and using media money to pound out persuasion and trial. New school is very different. Consumers are talking back. They want a brand they trust, with a purpose they believe in; a brand that reflects who they are, and that makes their life better and easier. And just for good measure, they also want fantastic products and flawless service.

Your brand is the sum of all the ideas that define your place in the world.

Consumers want to trust brands, but they are leery. That's because we have entered a "trust but verify" world. Consumers listen to Brand Promises, but don't trust them until brands deliver on those promises. Many companies are actually already consciously doing this and reaping the rewards. They realize that if you can do the difficult things to deliver on your promises consistently, consumers will trust you. As Jeff Bezos of Amazon says, "You earn reputation by trying to do the hard things well."

One of the hard things is actively defining and creating your brand, because if you don't do it, someone else will do it for you—either your consumers or your competition. When you think about brands that seem to have lost their way, the list gets long pretty quickly. While their problems may be for many reasons, Nokia, Nintendo, Avon, Nescafé, Dell, and JCPenny don't have brands that are helping them.

Three elements of a brand:

The Brand Promise—the value proposition/positioning of your product aligned to the values/purpose of your organization.

The Brand Personality—the unique style and character of the way you present your brand to the world

The Brand Identity—the integration of all the pieces of your brand into a cohesive whole

WE'RE ONLY HUMAN

A brand relationship is not unlike human relationships.

In the next section, we will breakdown *Brand Promise*, *Personality* and *Identity* into their component parts. But before we do, a useful notion to check the integrity of a brand is that a brand relationship is not unlike human relationships. People tend to use their personal relationships as a mental model for relationships with brands. Hence, the personification of brands with words like personality, character and identity. If you think about what you value in your personal relationships, it's honesty, consistency, predictability and shared values to name a few; your relationships with brands are no different.

A brand may not be a person, but today it has to act like a person.

Like people, when we meet brands, they can dazzle us with their looks and charm, but quickly we begin to look for substance and character. Add to this the deeper and more meaningful connection enabled by technology and social communities, and there's an expectation of trust and substance with brands that rarely existed in our more superficial past. A brand may not be a person, but today it has to act like a person: a good person with the qualities you would want in a trusted friend.

3. THE BRAND PROMISE

DO WHAT YOU SAY

The customer experience of a brand is the brand.

Every time any of us interacts with a brand, we are either in the process of receiving a brand's promise or experiencing it if it is being delivered. A Brand Promise describes what a customer can expect to get from a company. It is made up of both specific, quantifiable promises, and intangible promises. It reflects what the company believes in and stands for (its purpose and values), plus the value proposition of the product, and the differentiated position of the brand versus the competition, all packaged into an integrated and, hopefully, compelling story. Parts of it will change over time, but the foundation will not.

Gallup research finds that effective Brand Promises are:

Compelling: delivers an important and differentiated value proposition

Connecting: consistently connects emotionally with customers

Credible: fits the brand's identity

These promises are not just overt promises (although some can be), but they are impressions made every time someone interacts with a brand. The sum of these impressions tell us what to think, believe and expect.

A Brand Promise is a promise for a better future.

To continue the personification idea, the Brand Promise is the hope and expectation that a new friend creates. Let's say you're an enthusiastic, beginning rock climber. You meet someone with experience who offers to help you. He is friendly, a lover of the sport, just like you, and you both share a passion for the joys of the great outdoors. This is a new friend, someone with knowledge and experience you value, someone who shares your interests and passions, and someone you want to trust and believe in. It's the beginning of a relationship. Everyone has been in this position. What happens next is the difference between this new person turning out to be a genuine and valued friend, or a flake. It's the same with brands.

A Brand Promise is a promise for a better future. It creates an expectation that the product will make things better, in some large or small way. The trick is to make sure that the ideas that make up your promise are credible and meaningful to your target audience. People are assaulted by messages and media 24/7, so they need to believe before they will care and remember. Vague promises that feel like they cannot be experienced, evaluated or measured, like "We're the best!" are worthless. People are looking for brands that are confident enough to put themselves on the line in some way or another.

"Measure us against our promises" is a very powerful position to take.

Consumers are experts. They have been the recipients of marketing for years, and while they may not be technical experts, like marketers, they are experienced and confident enough to know what they want and expect from brands. What they are looking for is truth and authenticity, and it has a feel. Some say people can actually sense the truth of a company and if their commitments are real, or only on paper. Promises, therefore, cannot be made lightly. That's why you must build your brand on insights that come from evidence. Guessing is very dangerous, and flimflam rarely works for long. There is simply no alternative to truly understanding the behavior and psychology of your prospects and customers, your competition and your own organization.

4. BRAND PURPOSE & MISSION

START WITH THE WHY

People prefer brands associated with causes or their community.

Your purpose and mission are at the foundation of your Brand Promise. This is not to be confused with company values, which while important, are usually less differentiating. Your purpose is about why you are doing what you are doing. As Simon Sinek famously articulated, most companies start on the outside with "What" and then talk about "How." But companies that have really strong brands start from the inside with "Why." He explains that the "Why" of your company is not making profits, but the purpose of your organization. He argues that in the same way that we all want to be connected to ideas and movements that are greater than we are, organizations have to provide us with a larger purpose if they want our passionate commitment.

The "why" of your company is not making profits, but the purpose of your organization.

A brand's purpose is about the difference it makes, or is trying to make, in the world. Southwest Airlines staked out its purpose as "To connect people to what's important in their lives through friendly, reliable, and low-cost travel." They aligned their purpose and mission with their value proposition exactly. Walmart's promise, "Everyday low prices," later evolved to "Save money, live better," which is perfectly aligned with Sam Walton's founding purpose of helping people provide better lives for their families.

Consumers want to understand what a company stands for, so that they can decide if they want to stand with it. This is especially true of millennials and Generation Z (the post millennials). People raised to only know a digitally connected reality seem to have a more active and pronounced expectation that the companies they associate with have a reason for being that they can believe in. After almost ten years, Dove's campaign for Real Beauty has proven it has enduring resonance with millennials who yearn for authenticity. Warby Parker, an eyeglasses maker, hits the spot perfectly for millennials with the purpose: "For every pair purchased, a pair is distributed to someone in need."

WHAT'S THE BIG IDEA

Global spending on responsible products is huge and growing.

Defining a purpose is hard for most companies. Creating a mission statement is much easier and clear cut. According to the Harvard Business Review, a company mission "describes what business the organization is in (and what it isn't) both now and projecting into the future. Its aim is to provide focus for management and staff." American Express's mission is a good example of the clarity required: "American Express makes it easier, safer and more rewarding for customers and businesses to purchase the things they need."

Purpose is a more complex concept that speaks to a company's connection to its community, and its desire to effect change for the greater good. That change might be empowering small investors, which Charles Schwab set out to do, Red Bull's "Give wings to people and ideas," or Pampers purpose of "Caring for the happy, healthy development of babies."

It should be something that you can directly affect with your business.

Your brand's purpose needs to be a big idea, a dream, like Coke's "...to refresh the world and inspire moments of optimism and happiness." It should be a long-term, unchanging goal that consumers feel is important, and that inspires, motivates and gives your organization a reason to be. Your purpose doesn't necessarily have to be a cause, although most consumers say they prefer a company that pursues a cause they believe in. It should, however, be something that you can directly affect with your business. Unilever's purpose is to "make sustainable living commonplace," which they bring to life with a commitment to "reduce its [environmental] footprint to future-proof its supply base, reduce costs and provide direct benefits to consumers to help improve their health and well-being." This doesn't exactly trip off the tongue, but your purpose doesn't have to be a slogan or a memorable tag line, it just has to be real. The objective is to create a purpose that lives in everything your company does; one that's not just window dressing, but that is a genuine and meaningful goal of the organization. It should be easy to understand, and, of course, it helps if employees, and even consumers find it inspiring.

The idea is to inspire people, not make their eyes
glaze over.

Even in their purpose statement Nike can't resist its marketing urge. Adidas, on the other hand, is far more corporate and uninspiring.

Adidas — "The Adidas Group strives to be the global leader in the sporting goods industry with brands built on a passion for sports and a sporting lifestyle."

Nike — "To bring inspiration and innovation to every athlete* in the world.

*If you have a body, you are an athlete."

5. BRAND VALUES

HOW TO BEHAVE

Marketing today is about values.

Values are the way you live, and the way companies conduct themselves. They become important, not in the definition of your purpose or the setting of your mission, but in the day-to-day execution that determines success or failure. As we discussed at the beginning of this chapter, so much of the success of a brand is in how well it aligns its promise and its execution. Execution is the daily grind of making sure everything is done well. It takes determination and character, and that's where values come in. Values tell your employees and partners what's important in every situation. They provide the guidance your team needs to solve problems and confront new challenges. They become the scales that weigh the character of a company and, by extension its brands. Values are about the way you live and the way companies conduct themselves.

If your mission tells you where you are going, and your
purpose tells you why, your values tell you how to behave
along the way.

Patagonia's values are "Quality," "Integrity," "Environmentalism," and what they call "Not bound by convention." This translates into their integrated purpose and mission statement:

"Build the best product, cause no unnecessary harm, use business to inspire and implement solutions to the environmental crisis." Their values of "Quality" and "Not bound by convention" speak to their mission of building great products. The rest of the statement, however, is about their higher purpose and reflects their values of "Integrity" and "Environmentalism." But unlike so many of these exercises, Patagonia's values are not just words on paper. They are a living reality for the company and its consumers, proven with initiatives like their "Footprint Chronicles," which examines "Patagonia's life and habits as a company." Recently they announced: "The shells we make are contributing to climate change. Despite our best efforts to minimize this contribution, we are still part of the problem." This kind of honesty and integrity takes courage. Consumers see it and value it.

6. VALUE PROPOSITION

NOWHERE TO HIDE

If your product or service is not excellent and at minimum on par with your competition, the truth will quickly come out.

A brand's value proposition is the heart of its promise. If the product and what it can do isn't relevant to your target audience, your purpose, mission and values will not be either. In the recent past, brands could get away with inferior offerings because consumers had imperfect information. But the digital age has let consumers shine a light on every aspect of every product. The result is there is nowhere for brands to hide anymore. If your product or service is not excellent and at minimum on par with your competition, the truth will quickly come out. Job one for any company is, therefore, to ensure that your offering is at minimum competitive in quality. This is wonderful for consumers, but in itself has upset business-as-usual across the world of commerce.

Digital has let consumers shine a light on every aspect of every product.

At minimum, a value proposition has to be true now. It is the distillation of the benefits and value that a company promises to deliver to customers with a product or service. It answers the questions "What's in it for me?" and "Why should I buy this from you?" It is not a description of your business model; it's a clear, easy to understand, short statement about the product. If you have to do a lot of reading, or if you don't get it immediately, it's not working. When seeing or hearing a value proposition you should instantly know what it is, who it's for and why it's valuable.

Unlike your mission, purpose or values, your value proposition can change. It's not a tagline or slogan like Nike's *"Just Do It,"* because it defines the promise of your product very specifically.

Simple, clear value propositions:

CakeHealth:
"The best free way to manage healthcare. CakeHealth brings all your healthcare plans together online so you can easily track your healthcare spending without the paperwork."

Microsoft Office 365:
"Office 365 for your business. Get virtually anywhere access to the Microsoft Office tools you know and rely on, plus easy-to-administer business class IT services."

GEICO:
"15 minutes or less can save you 15% or more on car insurance."

Some might argue that this value proposition for GEICO is actually a slogan, which it is. But what it so artfully does is encapsulate the essence of their value proposition into a single, short, punchy sentence that serves as a slogan too. This is harder to do than it looks.

RELEVANT & COMPELLING

Target the value proposition to the needs and reality of the target consumer.

Most people research three to five options before making a product choice. This is when your value proposition needs to clearly set you apart. Value propositions are product specific and as quantifiable as you can make them while still being easy to consume. Clearly, the more targeted the value proposition is to the needs and reality of the target consumer, the better. This means that you may have variations on your value proposition for different target personas or different contexts. This can become an organizational challenge.

> **The more individually relevant a value proposition is, the more compelling it will be.**

Your value proposition should be:

Relevant—how it solves your problem or improves your life

Quantifiable—how it delivers specific benefits

Unique—why you should choose it versus something else

Value propositions are very important, and it is smart to test them to ensure they are resonating with their target audience before rolling them out. This can be as simple as A/B testing on your website, which is where you test and compare two different versions. You can even run a couple of Google AdWords campaigns to see which one delivers more clicks.

7. BRAND POSITIONING

KNOW YOUR PLACE

> **Showing what you are not helps to explain what you are.**

Reis & Trout wrote a seminal book back in 1980 called *Positioning: The Battle for Your Mind*. The premise was that consumers had limited space in their consciousness for brands, so for each category there would be brands that owned the key awareness slots. Brands would therefore have to position themselves versus their competitors in order to get a spot in a consumer's mind. Radio stations in the U.S. took this idea and ran with it. Stations were "Soft hits, without the hard rock" or "Rock without the sleepy stuff." It seemed that stations were forever finding narrower and narrower slices of the pie to try and own: "'70s oldies with commercial-free mornings and no hard rock afternoons."

Laying claim to a slice of the market helps the consumer understand what you do.

The idea of positioning today is similar in that laying claim to a slice of the market helps the consumer understand what you do, and positioning that claim against your competitor's makes it easier for consumers to understand your claim. Zipcar, for example, sees its competition as car ownership: "To urban-dwelling, educated techno-savvy consumers, when you use Zipcar car-sharing service instead of owning a car, you save money while reducing your carbon footprint." It can get complicated, and you should be careful not to build a position on a distinction without a difference. Your positioning doesn't have to be a separate consumer-facing statement, but should inform your general Brand Promise, for your internal team by clarifying your differentiation versus your competitors.

Great positioning statements:

- **Home Depot:** The hardware department store for doityourselfers.
- **Volvo:** For upscale American families, Volvo is the family automobile that offers maximum safety.
- **Target:** Style on a budget.

Consider how much is in the phrase "Style on a Budget." Style denotes an orientation towards fashion, a concern with design sensibilities and perhaps a promise of quality; at least as it is usually associated with style. Budget tells the viewer that prices are reasonable. Together they position the brand as for people who care about style but are careful with their money. This contrasts them against stores that sell style only, such as a department store, or those that sell budget only, such as, Kmart; in other words, Target is the "get it all" choice.

Your Brand Promise is a synthesis of all the information that your consumer wants to know, not only about your product, but about your character as a company. There are many permutations, some are more positioning statements, some more of a value proposition, and some are simple taglines. There are no hard and fast rules, except that what you say and how you behave with consumers should reflect all the choices you've made. A good Brand Promise, however, is still not enough. While a clear offering is important in this intensely competitive world, it's not, in most cases, compelling enough on its own.

8. BRAND PERSONALITY

WHO ARE YOU?

The way to passion is not through the mind but through the heart.

Just as people have their rational, analytical side and their emotional side, so do brands. When we first meet someone, all the visual and behavioral cues that we experience give us an impression of their personality. Then, over time, as we get to know them, our perceptions deepen. People respond to brands in a similar way.

There has been a great deal of research over the years on the subject of Brand Personality and why it seems to work. Research by Jennifer L. Aaker at Stanford in the late nineties found a pretty close correlation between the five generally recognized, human personality characteristics and the qualities that people imbue brands with, which brands are often quite happy to adopt. Her research found that the correlation wasn't quite one-to-one, and that certain qualities of Brand Personality were unique and derived from the aspirational effect of associating with brands. In other words, brands also had a unique ability to make us dream about what was possible in ourselves and our lives. The chart below shows the five human qualities that Aaker's research found were most associated with brands. *Sophistication* and *Ruggedness* are the two that speak most to aspirations and correlate more closely with brands than with people.

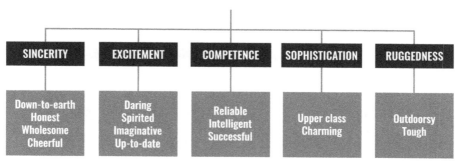

BRAND PERSONALITY

SINCERITY	EXCITEMENT	COMPETENCE	SOPHISTICATION	RUGGEDNESS
Down-to-earth Honest Wholesome Cheerful	Daring Spirited Imaginative Up-to-date	Reliable Intelligent Successful	Upper class Charming	Outdoorsy Tough

ARCHETYPES

According to Jung, archetypes are the primordial patterns that drive us all.

Another useful way to look at Brand Personality is *Brand Archetypes*. The idea, borrowed from famed psychologist Carl Jung, holds that there are universal, timeless personality types. If consumers relate to brands like people, the theory goes, then brands should model their personality on one of Jung's primary archetypes in order to take advantage of its built-in power.

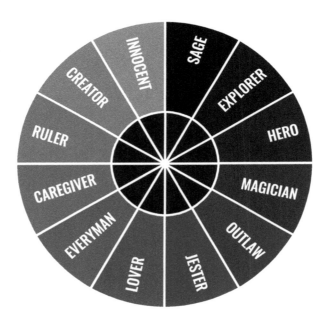

An analysis of 14,000 brands worldwide by BrandZ™ identified several archetypes that seem to be more successful for brands than others. They noticed that brands with certain archetypes tended to produce stronger brand equity. Interestingly they noted that the Top 100 brands, such as **IBM** or Microsoft, are most often "Sage Rulers."

There are generally four groupings of archetypes. Those that provide structure, those that reflect our yearning for bliss, those that speak to our need to leave our mark, and those about connecting with others. Whether you use this method or Aaker's, you should have a sense of the type of personality that will fit your brand from the strategic work you have already done. Recognizing that your choice of your Brand Personality will shape execution in everything you do in marketing, advertising, and how you interact with your customers—make sure you don't guess. Go through a methodical process and ensure that what you decide upon is aligned with the other aspects of your brand.

Explorer brands—Jeep, GoPro

Hero brands—FedEx, Nike

Creator brands—Apple, Adobe

9. BRAND EXPRESSION

LOOKS ARE ~~NOT~~ EVERYTHING

We live in an intensely visual world.

Once you have settled on a Brand Personality, you will need to consider how it is expressed. That starts with the visual expression of your brand, which is more than just selecting colors and shapes. It is an important exercise because the visual expression of your brand is a direct language, like music, that speaks emotionally to people with great meaning. There are no rules, except that your choices should incorporate and reflect all the ideas that make up your brand, integrated into a single authentic visual style that is consistent with your personality. For example, if your brand is dedicated to personal service, then it could visually reflect that with warmth and people. However, if your brand is about efficiency and reliability, it may have a cooler image, like IBM and many technology manufacturers.

Within a single picture a brand can tell its complete story or send entirely the wrong message.

The photography you choose, for example, is also very important. The style of the images, the way they are composed, the quality of the light, and, of course, what they feature, say important things about the nature of your Brand Personality. Consumers pick up on it. They might not always be conscious of all the small details that, hopefully, you have sweated over, but they respond emotionally to the aggregation of those many small impressions. The visual choices you make will create these emotional impressions, and, as such, need to be consciously aligned with your Brand Personality. This is especially important in our increasingly visual world where photography and videos seem to dominate media, and particularly social media. Within a single picture a brand can tell its complete story or send entirely the wrong message. GoPro, as you might hope, is good at using images. They feed a constant stream of videos and images out into the world that consistently capture the essence of their Brand Identity.

IT'S NOT WHAT YOU SAY

Everyone needs to understand how to communicate.

"Voice" denotes the style of communication, written or spoken, that a brand uses. There are as many styles as there are types of personality. The style of speaking, the words a brand chooses, says something about them, just as it would for a person. "Tone" is similar in that a creative manifestation of your brand, like a video, will have an overall tone, which might come from the music you select, or the overall creative approach used. All of these factors need to align with your Brand Personality. You cannot have a serious brand tone on your website and a light-hearted brand tone in your advertising. People will notice, and that inconsistency will leave an impression of inauthenticity. Every touchpoint should be part of this alignment and the consistency that it produces. This extends to even the scripts your customer service reps use, and the way they speak to customers.

Dollar Shave Club exploded from a combination of a strong, differentiated value proposition, combined with a personality that was original and authentic. The idea was to offer guys an easier, cheaper way to handle the whole shaving blade thing: "Dollarshaveclub.com—Our Blades are F***ing Great." The voice and tone were exceedingly clear and extended to the video that launched the brand. It has since continued to propel them to multiple bathroom products for guys, and the company is now approaching nine figures in sales.

Inconsistency will leave an impression of inauthenticity.

Once all of these elements have been decided, it's invaluable to produce a *Brand Style Guide*. The purpose of this document is to give everyone who might be creating marketing materials of any kind, from websites to TV commercials, clear direction on what fits the brand and what does not. It specifies the typefaces you use, the style of writing, the way the logo can be featured and much more. It's also useful to provide a version of this document to employees who will be directly communicating with customers and prospects. This should lay out all the choices you've made about Brand Personality and your greater identity so that anyone representing the company can understand what and how they need to communicate.

10. BRAND IDENTITY

THE TOUCHSTONE

Clearly communicate what your brand means to your people.

Identity is the totality of a brand. It encompasses everything we have talked about so far and is designed to keep the organization true to its brand. So far, we've seen how the *Mission* flows out of the *Purpose* and is kept alive with *Values*. We've seen how these unchanging ideas act as the foundation for the *Value proposition* and *Brand Positioning*, which shape the *Brand promise*. Finally, we've seen how the brand manifests itself with its *Personality* in the form of *Visual*, *Voice* and *Tone* expressions. Together all these pieces combine to form the *Brand Identity*. Your Brand Identity should become an internal touchstone that guides the understanding of what your brand means throughout your organization.

In his book *Strategic Brand Management* first published in 1992, Professor Jean-Noel Kapferer introduced a widely used model for brand identity. This model is made up of all the elements of the brand. Like the world we live in, however, it has necessarily evolved to reflect the relationship that brands have with consumers today.

Brand Prism

The Six Facets of Your Brand Identity:

Tangible Brand Promise

Consumers need to clearly understand what a brand does, why it is different and why it is better. This includes your *Value Proposition* and your *Brand Positioning*.

Brand Values

Similarly, the Brand Values are unchanging and guide employees as they create the experience of the brand every day.

Brand Purpose

This is the brand's higher purpose. It also includes the Brand Mission. The Brand Purpose is unchanging, but over time the brand's mission may shift as the world changes.

Customer Self-Image

The persona a brand shows in its marketing becomes the aspirational personification of the ideal user and the source for identification with the brand. Brands need to understand the cultural context that drives these aspirations.

Shared Values

In this socially aware world brands need to understand the values that they share with their community of customers.

Brand Personality

The *Visual Brand* plus *Voice & Tone* are an expression of your *Brand Personality*. This is where Aaker's *Brand Personality Framework* and *Brand Archetypes* come into play.

11. BRAND ESSENCE & PILLARS

RALLYING CRY

Create a mantra to inspire your organization.

In the center of the Identity Prism is the *Brand Essence*. This is the synthesis of all the aspects of the prism. It is useful because it distills the essential ideas from each perspective represented by the six sides of the prism into a simple rallying cry to guide and inspire your organization. *Brand Essence* is not usually a consumer-oriented statement, like a slogan that can change, but instead doesn't change because it represents your brand's unique place in the world.

It needs to be unchanging, consistently true and authentic across your entire brand eco-system.

Creating a Brand Essence statement is not easy. You have to incorporate the consumer's unique and meaningful emotional experience of your brand into just a couple of words. The shorter and more focused it is, the more powerful it will be, such as Hallmark's "Caring shared." Then, when you have settled on your rallying cry, it needs to be unchanging, consistently true and authentic across your entire brand eco-system.

Brand Essence:

- **Nike:** Authentic Athletic Performance
- **Disney:** Fun Family Entertainment
- **The Nature Conservancy:** Saving Great Places

STAYING FOCUSED

Directives for employees to live by.

After doing all this work to define your brand and integrate it into a Brand Identity, you don't want it to sit on a shelf somewhere. While the Brand Essence is valuable as an internal rallying cry, it is not an actionable daily guide for your organization. That's where your *Brand Pillars* come in.

Brand Pillars become directives that the company should live by.

Brand Pillars are short statements that can clearly guide your organization in all its consumer interactions and keep them aligned with the overall Brand Identity. They do not necessarily drive specific marketing messages, but rather help focus employees on what's important. Since so much of a brand's success today is determined by its ability to enlist its employees in bringing the brand to life, Brand Pillars become directives that the company should live by. The fewer the pillars you have, the easier it will be for your team to make sure they happen.

Hilton:

Brand Purpose:
- To fill the earth with the light and warmth of hospitality.

Brand Mission:
- To be the preeminent global hospitality company.
- The first choice of guests, team members, and owners alike.

Brand pillars:
- A clean, smart room for me.
- Nourish me in new and exciting ways.
- Meet my needs especially if I have a problem.
- Respect and value me and my loyalty.
- Show me you care.

12. BRAND STORY

HOW WE'RE WIRED

Great brands tell great stories.

While the brand creation process requires creative thinking, it is not a creative process in and of itself. Most of the creative work is done as you activate the brand and take it to market. However, it is also important to be conscious, even at this early stage, of the power of stories.

The human condition is about stories. Our cultural memories are stories handed down. Our personal lives are stories told and retold. Our very humanity is explained and understood with stories.

We are programmed to think, remember and decipher the world with stories.

As you create your Brand Identity it is important to think in terms of stories. We all share in the arc of life and its common experiences, and our stories invariably reflect these timeless truths. The authenticity that a brand should strive for can therefore only be enhanced by shaping it into a story that resonates on an archetypal human level.

Guinness tells stories where consumers can identify with the characters and values they hold. One commercial shows a bartender who leaves a pint of Guinness at an empty table every night. Night after night the table remains empty and the barmaid scares off anyone eyeing the empty chairs. We don't know who it's for until at last, a soldier returns home to find his Guinness waiting for him. The commercial ends with the line "The choices we make reveal the true nature of our character."

Brand stories take many shapes and forms. One of the most familiar, and perhaps powerful, is the brand tagline. When many people think about branding they not only think logos, but also taglines. That's because taglines are one of the ways we remember brands. They are representative of the Brand Identity you craft, but the tagline usually captures only part of the brand idea. Taglines can lean towards any of the fundamental brand attributes, but more often than not they reflect positioning of one type or another. Despite that, the best taglines contain the essence of the brand story.

Famous Taglines:

- **U.S. Army:** Be all you can be
- **Miller Lite:** Great Taste, Less Filling
- **Budweiser:** For all you do, this Bud's for you
- **Burger King:** Have it your way
- **Avis:** We're #2. We try harder

13. BRAND STRATEGY

DIGITAL FIRST

The internet changed everything.

The way brands come alive today, often called brand activation, has changed with the digital age. So much of a brand's interactions with consumers are now in digital channels, with digital experiences at the heart of the consumer relationship. This calls for a digital-first approach in thinking about how a brand can be valuable to its consumers.

Be sensitive to the digital reality of your consumers' lives.

While an agnostic, consumer-centric approach to strategy and branding is always the right way to go, the reality is that most products and services today are digitally centered in their interactions with their consumers. So, it's only smart to be thinking about how to bring the value of the brand to life in digital channels from the outset. This often means using technology to solve consumer problems, remove barriers to happiness, enable effortless convenience, and to look for innovative ways to re-invent the consumer experience in your category. The results of this mindset will enable your brand strategy to be sensitive to the digital reality of your consumers' lives. That's why having the insights of sophisticated digital strategists and marketers as part of the brand creation process is indispensable.

BUILD YOUR ECO-SYSTEM

Make it easy to stay relevant and connected to your consumers.

The importance of a strong brand in today's world is greater than ever before. The good news is that the investment required to create your brand and bring it to life is considerably less than what you would have to invest if you were to rely on advertising alone.

The new rules of the marketing world shift the focus from ads to creating a digital brand eco-system that you can own. This is done with websites, social media sites, content and other digital assets that are still not cheap but that are not "here today, gone tomorrow" like advertising. Unlike advertising, the digital infrastructure that you need to make a modern brand eco-system will last for some time. With it, you have the chance to stay connected to your consumers, so you don't have to reacquire them over and over again. This underscores the case for a shift from paid media to investing in your brand.

Digital infrastructure makes a modern brand eco-system work.

The process we've outlined above will give you all the elements you need to have a healthy brand. However, as with all strategic work, it will not mean much without excellent execution, which begins with the subject of the next chapter.

CHAPTER 3

HELLO WORLD

Connect with consumers for the first time

EXECUTIVE SUMMARY

- Introducing your brand to the world may still require some good old-fashioned advertising to get things started.
- The good news is that the digital age has created the possibility for brands to spend less on paid advertising and more on their own direct channels to consumers.
- Once a brand gets momentum within their community of customers, the potential for organic growth without the big media costs is terrific.
- Until then, brands should use a mix of Brand Advertising, made up of Branding campaigns and Direct Response campaigns, plus Brand Activation, which are tactics that leverage *Owned* channels such as your website.

Introducing your brand to the world:

- **Brand Advertising**
  - Brand campaigns establish value for the brand with new prospects. Brands need to establish their value before trying to close the deal.
  - Since consumers do research online, it frees advertising up to focus on attracting attention emotionally.
  - Direct response campaigns focus on a call-to-action. They typically work better once the value of a brand is established.

- Paid and organic search is a direct response channel that can attract in-market prospects early. But those people will still need to be cultivated before they buy.

- **Media Planning & Buying**
  - Buying media today is a complex business. You don't need to understand all of it, but you should know the basics. Make sure you have a good partner.
  - Media, especially digital media, has become very measurable. This allows you to set marketing goals and measure performance against those goals.
  - The analysis of what the metrics mean gives you invaluable insights.
  - Data can tell a brand what's working and what's not. With nearly real-time metrics from almost everything a brand does, it is possible to constantly optimize and improve performance.

- **Brand Activation**
  - This includes all the awareness and acquisition tactics possible through *Owned* and *Earned* media.
  - Tactics include making content, which can be found by search, and can be shared.
  - Influencer marketing to harness consumers as well as influential people in social media.
  - Relationship marketing to leverage your customer's good will in social media and ratings and reviews.
  - Experiential marketing using events to introduce your brand and make it come to life.

- **Creativity**
  - Creativity becomes important as you take your brand out into the world.
  - You want your brand to be unique in the minds of your consumers.
  - Originality and big ideas in marketing can be enormously valuable.
  - Creativity is challenging for conservative organizations.

HELLO WORLD

Connect with consumers for the first time.

This book is constructed so each chapter builds on the previous chapter. In Chapter 1 we outlined the strategic planning process that a brand needs to go through. This results in a *Playbook* of tactics for 12–24 months and a *Roadmap* outlining the long-term vision for your brand's eco-system and infrastructure. Chapter 2 builds on this by exploring how to create your brand. This covers all the elements that make up a strong, modern brand. Underlying this strategic planning and brand strategy should be your business strategy, which precedes them. Assuming that all of this work is done, you will not only have a well-constructed brand and a solid plan in place, but also most of the answers you need as you prepare to connect with consumers for the first time.

No matter what you are selling, it has to start somewhere, so the subject of this chapter is that initial connection with consumers. While, as you will see, some of the dynamics of this process are new, much is the way it used to be. This is important in the context of the *Considered Purchase* because this initial connection is the step that sets up the consideration process, which we will cover in Chapter 4. As we have discussed, one of the big changes in marketing is the improved capability of consumers to fully evaluate all the aspects of a potential purchase. Before that can happen, however, brands have to first reach out and get their attention.

As we described in the last chapter, aligning your delivery with the promise you make is critical to success, assuming you have an offer people care about. But before you can prove your promise is true, you first need to communicate it. That starts with *Brand Advertising* and *Brand Activation*, which present your Brand Promise to your target audience.

Before you can prove your promise is true, you first need to communicate it.

Getting awareness and sales used to be pretty straightforward. Brands had their advertising agency create ads and then buy media. The focus was mostly on the creativity involved, since the number of media options was limited. The ads themselves were much more important than they are today because they had to do most of the heavy lifting, not only creating awareness, but also by presenting much of the value proposition. While this simpler world hasn't been around for almost a generation now, many people still think this is the way things work. Today, however, the challenge is much more complex, like everything else in marketing, and paid media advertising is only one piece of the puzzle.

REVISITING THE JOURNEY

Getting the marketing process going.

Whereever your brand sits on the awareness continuum today, from completely unknown to a household name, you need to create awareness with your prospects as a first step in getting the marketing process going. If you are already well known, then the challenge might be to move into a new audience segment. If you are starting out and your target consumers don't know your brand exists, then nothing else much will happen until you change that. In order to understand how to do this, we first need to take another look at the consumer journey.

Create awareness as a first step in getting your story out.

As we outlined in Chapter 1, consumers go on a journey. We used to think of it as a one-way journey with the funnel metaphor. Now we think of it more as a circular journey, starting with a trigger point, going through to purchase, and then looping around into loyalty and advocacy.

The Stage of the Consumer Journey:
- **Trigger**—What causes a consumer to begin thinking about a purchase?
- **Consideration**—Is this purchase necessary and feasible? What will it mean?
- **Evaluation**—Which product is better and why?
- **Purchase**—How and where is the purchase completed? Why should you buy now? Is it easy?
- **Loyalty**—What is the experience of the product? Will customers become advocates?

The trigger stage starts the ball rolling. The job at this stage is simply to get your brand on the awareness radar of your target audience. Unlike in days gone by, you don't have to also make the entire pitch and close the deal at the same time, which should be a big relief. That's because the consumer's approach to buying has changed.

HOW WE BUY

Leverage the natural process that we all go through.

Think about how you buy just about anything. First you decide you have a need. That may be because of a genuine need, or because marketing helps you identify a need you didn't know you had. Let's say you get inspired to start thinking about buying a convertible car. The initial trigger might be an ad, a social post, a viral video or just seeing a good-looking car drive by. It may spark your interest in the category, or it may even start you leaning toward a particular brand. This first step usually only sets the emotional stage. It doesn't push you directly into evaluation and purchase, but rather into a gentle education process where you are exploring the possibilities and what they might mean for you. This is the consideration phase. You start to dream about what owning a convertible would be like, you explore models online, and begin to learn what your options are. Then, at some point, the magic moment arrives when desire, need and capability align. You get a bonus at work; finally you have enough money. Now you get serious. You probably already have some convertible brands in mind. You may even have your dream car all spec'd out. You enter the evaluation mode, and your analytical skills come to the fore as you weigh your options, make your selection and prepare to negotiate a deal.

Make that initial connection with the target consumer by creating the trigger that starts things off.

What's left out of this story of how a consumer gets to the point of making a purchase is the brand's side. Numerous influences can affect consumer perceptions along the way, and today many are from brands. From the brand's perspective, the process is one of *Connecting, Cultivating* and *Converting*. Selling has always happened in these stages, but today the dynamics have changed considerably. In this chapter, our focus is on *Connecting*; making that initial contact with the target consumer by creating the trigger that starts things off.

Two approaches:

Brand Advertising—This includes advertising campaigns, both brand campaigns, which shape the perception of the brand, and direct response campaigns, including search, which are designed to drive sales activity.

Brand Activation—This includes all of the other experiences you can create to engage your prospects, from a mobile app or retail event to a viral video.

2. BUDGETING

METHOD OVER MADNESS

Get the right budget to deliver your goals.

Brand Advertising and Brand Activation cost money and include many potential channels and choices. But before you can start to decide what to spend, you need to know how big your budget is. Your marketing plan process (Chapter 1) should have identified your marketing goals, and the tactics that were most likely to accomplish them. As part of that process you should also have estimated the associated costs and projected performance of those tactics in order to prioritize them. This now becomes the basis for your campaign budgeting.

You need to know how big your budget is.

If you haven't gone through this process, then you should quantify your goals for the year or the time period you're looking at and determine how much you can spend to achieve them. If your goal is to increase sales by 20%, you need to understand what the marginal value of those sales are and how much can be invested to reach them in order to deliver the required ROI. This calculation may also be influenced by other considerations, such as increasing share of market, or investing in the long-term value of an acquired customer. Either way, this will give you an amount of money to invest in order to achieve your goal. Within the highly measurable world that marketing has

become today, this sets up your activities to be like any other business investment; expected to deliver a specified and measurable return on investment.

Another way to approach budgeting is to start with the end in mind.
Decide how many sales you want to make and work backward through the
funnel to determine how many prospects have to go in the top, and what you
can afford to pay to get them. To do this successfully your assumptions about
conversion rates at each stage of the funnel have to be valid, conservative and
based on evidence. You also have to consider that since your *Paid* advertising
will be working with other *Owned* and *Earned* tactics, the budget will also have
to provide for their costs.

TYPICAL SPENDS

Competitive marketing is still not cheap.

According to the 2015 CMO survey, B2C companies with revenues over
$25mm spend around 9% of revenues on marketing, while B2B companies
spend around 8%. This not only covers advertising spend, but staffing, CRM,
content costs, etc. Interestingly if you study the fastest growing midsize and
large companies, many spend much more than this. In 2014, for example,
Salesforce spent 53% of its total revenue, LinkedIn 35%, Microsoft 18% and
even Tempur & Sealy, the bedding company, spent 21%! Those are very big
numbers, but it's fair to note that these companies also routinely produce
outsized year-on-year growth.

Companies that invest heavily in marketing do better than those that don't.

Of course, there are no hard-and-fast rules. But typically, companies that
invest heavily in marketing do better than those that don't, everything else being even. That's why some of the world's most valuable companies are the best
marketers: a look at the Forbes top 20 most valuable brands is a who's who of
brilliant marketers, featuring Coca-Cola, Apple, Disney, Toyota, McDonald's,
Nike, Mercedes and Samsung among others. That said, it's understandable
that business leaders, especially in smaller companies, are hesitant when they
leave the comparative comfort of their own business and venture into the less
predictable world of marketing. Unfortunately, however, the time has passed

when companies of almost any size, can avoid this discomfort and bypass marketing. The expectations of the digitally savvy consumer, combined with a highly competitive environment, mean that being good at marketing is now essential for success and even survival.

GO FOR THE JUGULAR

The power of an idea is stronger than the size of a budget.

Coming out of your marketing planning process, you should have identified the target audiences, media channels and the messaging approach you will use to connect with your prospects and customers. Some of these will be Brand Advertising, or *Paid* media channels, and some will be Brand Activation channels (many already part of your *Owned* and *Earned* media activities). Now, as you reach out to your target prospects for the first time, you will be focused on the channels and media outlets you have already identified as the best potential initial connection points.

There are two basic kinds of advertising campaigns that you can run: a *Brand* campaign or a *Direct Response* campaign. A brand campaign establishes value for your product or service, as compared to a direct response campaign, which is more suited to driving sales. Of course, everyone just wants sales, but it's important to remember that establishing perceived value for your brand is the necessary foundation before sales can happen. Of course, advertising is rarely clear-cut. Some campaigns combine branding elements with direct response and many direct response campaigns reinforce branding elements.

Brand campaigns can now focus and go straight for the emotional jugular.

Regardless, the basic role of a brand campaign is to create perceived value for the brand. If you've never heard of a product or don't have any opinions about it, you're not likely to buy it. Brand campaigns are all about presenting the Brand Promise and beginning to tell the brand story. It's the difference between a Ford ad that tells the story of their F-150 truck, and another F-150 ad that offers 0% financing. If you already have an impression of value for the F-150 then you are more likely to respond to a financing offer. Conversely, if you have no opinion about the F-150, then a discount deal is not likely to move you.

Traditionally, brand campaigns have used media like TV and print for branding. These mediums are good at creating emotional impressions, not only for those actively searching for solutions, but more importantly for those not even thinking about it yet. Before the digital age, when consumers were given the ability to do research easily, a great deal of our intention to buy came from these branding campaigns. But today, with digital channels handling most of the consideration process, brand campaigns have been untethered. They are now free to go straight for the emotional jugular, focusing on the emotional part of the formula without worrying so much about the analytical side of the sale. When the Queensland Board of Tourism wanted to get attention, it advertised for candidates for the "Best Job in the World:" six months taking care of a gorgeous little island off the Great Barrier Reef. They used a big idea to capture the emotional imagination of their target audience without diluting it with detail and selling. Using newspaper ads and social media the Board got over seven million visitors and 34,000 applicants for the job. This was a good example of how the power of an idea can be more powerful than the size of a budget.

PAY ATTENTION

Ads are now free to be arresting and original.

Consumers will go to the internet to research their options one way or another, so the idea is to create brand awareness and preference before they do. Most people need to be engaged emotionally before they are willing to invest time analytically, which is why ads need to capture our imagination, get us to dream, create desire, and lay down a foundation of positive feelings. But before an ad can do that, it first needs to get our attention.

Consumers don't have to pay attention anymore.

People are no longer captive audiences for ads. With on-demand TV and digital recorders, as well as Netflix, Hulu and the like, consumers have lost much of their tolerance for ads. And in digital channels most of us don't pay much attention to ads either because we've learned how to mentally screen them out. This makes original, emotionally arresting creativity a necessity if brands want to cut through consumer defenses and get them to pay attention. It's simple: We don't mind being entertained with funny commercials, just don't try to sell us anything.

Of course, if your prospect is actively looking and ready to buy, then any related ad will probably get their attention without having to emotionally engage them too much. For most products, this rarely represents more than a tiny percentage of the audience at any moment in time. While this small group will be easily hooked, the rest of the audience will probably not. Instead, they will first need to be enticed. They will need you to create emotional engagement and value for your brand before they will give it their trust.

Unfortunately, this isn't always what happens. Human nature being what it is, somebody in the leadership says, "We need sales now!" which results in marketing charging after that tiny sliver of ready to buy prospects again. If a brand hasn't already created strong brand preference, this usually wastes the majority of every advertising dollar invested. Focusing on people who are ready to buy, without that strong brand foundation in place, means you have to compete on things like price and promotions. This in turn forces you into a repetitive cycle of expensive acquisition tactics. What makes more sense is to use expensive advertising sparingly as part of a brand-building effort, and then to use digital channels, such as the brand website, to convert those ready to buy, and capture interested-but-not-quite-ready prospects into a cultivation process.

A GOOD START

Identify the best channels and media vehicles to reach your target audiences.

Brand Advertising channels include traditional media, such as TV, radio, print and outdoor, plus digital channels, such as digital advertising and acquisition email. These are all ways to trigger the beginning of consumer awareness. Deciding if a medium is the right one at this stage of the game is about answering a series of questions about your target consumers as part of your strategic planning process. Your work in developing your marketing plan will have identified the best channels and media vehicles to reach your target audiences at various points in their journey. This may include some traditional channels, such as TV, but things are changing. Digital channels continue to grab more consumer engagement every day, growing to almost 50% in 2017 according to eMarketer. At the same time TV use, the second biggest category, continues its slow slide. Despite that, TV and other traditional media remain powerful advertising channels when appropriate.

Replace *Paid* media with *Owned* and *Earned* media.

Using *Paid* media for Brand Advertising is still very expensive, so the idea is to use it as sparingly as possible. The good news is that the digital age has brought with it the opportunity to replace *Paid* media with less expensive *Owned* and *Earned* media. This enables brands to leverage content, customers and communities to get awareness, which we will discuss in the next chapter. It also means that, in general, brands should maximize the potential of their *Owned* media, such as their website, content, and their *Earned* media, such as social media, before turning to *Paid* media. Exceptions to this are when a brand has not built advocacy momentum with its customers and still needs to introduce itself and its Brand Promise to target consumers, or when a brand simply needs to add new consumers faster than it can get them organically. In these situations, *Paid* media can act as the accelerator to get the process going. This is when *Paid* media can attract attention, make the initial connection, start to create brand preference, and drive prospects to digital channels for the rest of the process. It's expensive compared to lower cost, slower, more organic alternatives, but when you need results quickly it may be necessary. The other use for *Paid* media is goosing sales with promotions, which we will talk about in Chapter 5.

4. DIRECT RESPONSE CAMPAIGNS

TAKING ACTION

Most digital advertising has been direct response so far.

The second type of Brand Advertising is called *Direct Response*. It is technically any ad that is designed to elicit a measurable response. However, now that almost all advertising is measurable, that distinction is less relevant. A better definition is that it's an ad that is designed to lead directly to a sales action. That might be a banner ad that sends you to a landing page where you can watch a video, or a TV spot with a toll-free number to call. Basically, a direct response ad is any ad designed to get the consumer to take an action that begins the sales cultivation process.

When introducing new ideas, start with brand campaigns.

The degree to which a brand can use direct response techniques is really a function of the offering and the situation. If your ad is giving away new cars for free, it wouldn't need much of a branding foundation to get a response. A good rule of thumb is if your audience consists of people who are already actively interested in your category, direct response can work. However, if you are introducing new ideas, new products, or new brands, you have to start with brand campaigns.

PAID SEARCH

The vast majority of shoppers use search for research before buying.

Perhaps the most unique form of direct response advertising is Search. Most people understand the concept, but it bears repeating. When you search for a word or phrase on Google you are presented with *organic* (also known as *natural*) search results. You are also presented with *paid* search results, which are often called *SEM* or *search engine marketing*. Google not only reinvented our lives with search, but with AdWords, its paid search advertising platform, it reinvented advertising itself.

With AdWords, its paid search advertising platform, Google reinvented advertising itself.

With paid search, the idea is to rank at the top of the results, so the viewer sees you first. Best of all, you only pay if someone clicks your ad. Ranking of paid search results is determined by who offers the most money for a potential click. Therefore, if you buy the search term "auto insurance" and bid more for a click than anyone else, then when someone types in "auto insurance," your company's ad will come up at the top of the paid search results. Since everybody conducts searches for almost everything they buy, paid search is an essential part of presenting your brand to prospects already actively looking.

ORGANIC SEARCH

The top three natural search results get most of the clicks.

Organic search results are not paid but earned. They are even more valuable than paid results because they are not ads and feel, therefore, more credible and trustworthy. According to Enquisite, organic search results are 8.5 times more likely to be clicked than paid results. Google works very hard to constantly improve the quality of the results they deliver for each inquiry; that's so that the search results we all get will be as relevant and valuable as possible. This is how Google secures its own value. They also work hard to fend off the hordes of search experts trying to manipulate the system to their advantage every day—although gaming the system is becoming less of a factor today as Google evolves its algorithms.

Organic search results, like paid search, are a great way to get "found" by people actively looking for a solution. In general, they are less effective for introducing new ideas or brands, but with a little creativity, organic searches can be made to work for introductions too. Getting to the top of the organic listings involves a combination of quality content and good SEO (search engine optimization). Rankings are determined by things like the number of other sites that link to your content, or the number of times that people have shared it. These are measures of quality, which is another way to say how important the content is to the audience. SEO is the process you use to make your content more likely to be found and ranked highly by the search engines, which send automated programs, called spiders, to crawl around the internet 24/7 looking for content to rank. Together, paid and organic searches have become basic building blocks of modern marketing. There is a lot to know about both and it's easy to get lost in the minutiae. The important thing to remember, however, is that today search is ultimately all about how good your content is. Great content gets found, ranked highly and shared; ordinary content does not. We will talk more about SEO and content throughout this book because it is one of the pieces of the puzzle you must master.

Search is amazing, but only if it connects intelligently to the rest of your marketing system.

Search is a fundamental part of any modern marketing plan, but it only works if it is connected to a marketing system. It's like being a door-to-door salesman. When someone answers the door, you've got to be ready with your pitch and your samples. Similarly, when you click on a search result, it should be just the beginning of the sales cultivation process. This is particularly important to remember at this stage of the game when the prospect probably doesn't yet have a predisposition towards your brand. For search to work it must be supported by a comprehensive cultivation system, designed to turn initial interest into qualified consideration and then conversion, as we will discuss in the next chapter. Search is amazing, but only if it connects intelligently to a smart marketing system.

5. MEDIA PLANNING & BUYING

THE BASICS

This is one of those areas where it is easy to get overwhelmed and confused.

Since Brand Advertising is often *Paid* media of one sort or another, this is an appropriate time to talk about media planning and buying. While you don't need to understand every nut and bolt yourself, you need to have a general familiarity with the basics, so you can direct the work. It's also wise to have access to someone you trust with deep knowledge on the subject, since this is one of those areas where it is easy to get overwhelmed and confused. Yes, there are hundreds of technologies, platforms, methods, vehicles and metrics in the media planning and buying world, but it's the fundamentals that you really need to understand. This is definitely a case where you need to see the forest.

You don't need to understand every nut and bolt yourself.

If you are not familiar with the practice of media planning and buying, the basics are pretty straightforward. The planner decides what media vehicles you should use. The buyer then negotiates the best deal with the media outlet. Both work together to monitor the performance of the media buy and hold the media outlet accountable for any performance guarantees they have made.

WHAT SHOULD YOU PAY?

Find a fee model that works for you.

In the early days of advertising, ad agencies were generally paid a fee of 15% of the entire media budget to perform planning and buying services. This also usually covered the cost of making the ads. Today, fees for media planning and buying are still usually a percentage of the media budget and run around 12%, getting lower as the budget gets larger. The fee does not, however, pay for creative or any other services anymore. This is because the amount and complexity of creative assets required has increased so much since the print days, that 15% rarely covers the cost of all the work required. A digital ad campaign, for example, may need dozens of different ads for different audiences and ad sizes. As a result, the percentage model can act as a disincentive for agencies to save their clients' money. To prevent that, you can use a fixed fee or hourly rate for the services involved.

It's important to have the same team that is creating the strategy be part of media planning.

Some years ago, the media team was separated from the creative team in many large advertising agencies, and media-only agencies were formed. The idea was that since the two cultures were very different, it would allow both to focus on their specialties. That trend, however, didn't anticipate how creative the media function itself would need to become in our more complex marketplace. As a result, there has been a reverse trend where media agencies are adding creative capabilities, and creative agencies are building media teams again. Today, for most brands, it's important to have the two functions working hand-in-hand. The same organization or agency that is creating the strategy and developing the creative, needs to closely influence the media planning process, although not necessarily the buying. This ensures that the right hand knows what the left is doing, and that the originality that is possible in designing a media plan syncs closely with the creativity and overall strategy of the campaign. In agencies where strategy is important, this works well because there is a natural fit between strategy and media planning.

PROGRAMMATIC BUYING

Projections say programmatic will soon gobble up most buying.

Buying is a process of negotiation, and depending on how much media you are buying, it may make sense to have a media buying specialist do the work for you. In some instances, large media buyers have more pricing leverage based on the volume of business they bring to bear from multiple clients. However, with the advent of programmatic buying, which is sort of like Google AdWords for media, the clout of an individual buyer or firm is becoming less.

Jimmy Kimmel called Programmatic Buying the "gluten" of advertising because everybody is talking about it, but few really understand what it is.

Programmatic Buying basically describes all the technologies that have been introduced to automate the process of buying and selling media. It covers most digital display and search paid media, and now includes video ads online and even on cable. It's like pricing and buying airline tickets on a website: fast, simple, and no travel agent required. That's why many larger brands have been bringing it in-house.

Some Programmatic Buying is *Real-time bidding* (RTB) just like an auction on eBay, and some of it is *Direct* or *Guaranteed*, in which you buy media directly from the publisher (versus from a network) and is similar to the Buy It Now feature on eBay. All of it is subject to the fraud "crisis," as the IAB chairperson called it, that has plagued digital advertising in recent years. This is where digital display ads register bogus views. According to the Wall Street Journal it turns out that as much as 50% of digital ad viewing has actually been done by robotic programs or bots. Needless to say, the digital advertising community has been wringing their hands as they have tried to get this threat to their credibility under control.

Tips about Media Buying:

While you will probably not do the buying in-house, here are a couple of hard-won insights about planning and buying media we've learned over the years that might be useful:

- There are a million media outlets, and they all have good stories. What you should care about are the audience numbers. Not *their* numbers, but independently verified numbers.
- Don't fall in love with the magazine, website, or program, focus on the audience.
- Make sure the media audience you buy closely aligns with your target audience. Adults 18–49 is more of a family reunion than a target audience.
- Care about context and timing. Think about what your target audience is thinking and doing when a media outlet reaches them.
- All ad slots in a TV show or on a webpage are not created equal.
- Make sure you have the right metrics. Impressions are mostly a useless measure.
- Monitor performance like a hawk.
- Always have minimum performance and placement guarantees, plus some form of structure to compensate you for under-delivery.
- The price is always negotiable, even if it's "sold out."

6. ANALYTICS

ART & SCIENCE

The importance of data has made good marketing analytics essential.

Every action we take on a digital device is measurable, hopefully anonymously, but measurable nevertheless. That has turned marketing from the unreliable stepson of business into the golden-haired child. There has always been a need to measure the performance of advertising, which produced Nielsen ratings for TV, Arbitron for radio, and the Audit Bureau of Circulation for print. Digital measurability, however, has restructured our expectations to believe we should be able to fully understand the effect of every marketing dollar we spend. While we are closer, this is not yet true, and measurement still remains a combination of art and science.

Measurement still remains a combination of art and science.

The science is in measuring activity. We can and do that with everything, especially digital marketing. The art is in picking the right measures to pay attention to and then drawing the correct conclusions. Setting KPIs (key performance indicators), which are important to the business, is essential. Sales, of course, is the ultimate KPI, but connecting marketing metrics to off-line sales is still a trick. Invariably, there is a tracking gap between marketing activity and the sale itself. This can misrepresent the influence of any particular channel on the sale. A growing solution is multi-touch attribution. This is the methodology of assigning weighted credit to the ad touches which lead to a conversion. How important was the last touch? How did previous touches play a part? Although still very imperfect, it will be influential in the future and is preferable to only giving credit to the last thing someone sees. It may also give us new insights into the layering effects of multi-touch marketing, which goes well beyond ads to content and digital.

THE VALUE CHAIN

Almost all advertisers are wasting money on advertising.

In paid digital advertising there are numerous metrics. A sampling includes impressions or cost per thousand (CPM), unique visitors, click through rate (CTR), cost per click (CPC), cost per lead (CPL), percentage complete, and time spent viewing. There are many more. The idea is to figure out the type of behavior that gets closest to inferring the outcome you want from the campaign. For example, a pure brand campaign, designed to create awareness and brand favorability, might focus on the time a prospect spent viewing a landing page, which they arrived at by clicking an ad. This would tell you the degree to which the prospect was interested and engaged, which we might infer would result in an increase in brand awareness and favorability. While these metrics would not directly measure sales or intent to purchase, they would give us an indication of the effectiveness of our brand engagement effort.

Many touches layer on and interact with each other until the consumer is ready to act.

Advertising and marketing today, however, are not a series of isolated activities, instead they are part of a marketing value chain in which many touches layer on and interact with each other until the consumer is ready to act. Just like Chinese water torture, we believe that one drop will finally do the trick, we just don't know which one. For that reason, the KPIs we select for any tactic should reflect the step in the consumer journey that the campaign is addressing. So, while a brand awareness campaign, at the beginning of the journey, would measure engagement, a demand generation campaign (later in the journey) would measure conversion.

Teams should produce weekly campaign reports that not only show activity metrics, but also performance against KPI goals. These are often best integrated into dashboards so that business leaders can see the greater meaning from consolidated data from across all your marketing activity. Traditional research is also still a valuable tool to determine important psychological measures such as brand recall or purchase intent, which are difficult to measure with activity metrics. Once again, these insights are still a couple of steps from connecting to sales but get you closer. If your target audience shows solid brand awareness, brand preference and intent to purchase, you know you are on track to get conversions.

Resist, however, the temptation to just look at sales for the period and think: if sales go up the marketing worked; and if sales go down, the marketing didn't work. The problem is that while there is probably truth in this, it does not enable a marketing organization to become smarter and more effective over time by learning. The only way to do that is to know which parts of your marketing are working and why, so that you can improve your performance.

MEDIA MIX

What is the optimum combination of media channels?

Media planning is a lot about numbers: audience estimates, sales projections, costs, ROI etc. In this age of data, it lends itself to attention from the quants. That's why *Media Mix Modeling* or MMM has become popular with many sophisticated marketers. MMM is an econometric process that uses marketing and sales data models to predict sales based on different combinations of brand advertising and activation tactics.

Many common assumptions about how each type of media works best seem to be generally correct.

You may or may not want to invest in this specialized approach to model your media decision-making, but the good news is that it has shown that many common assumptions about how each type of media works best seem to be generally correct. One large study by Google and GFK across 36 brands looked at numerous different combinations of media and concluded, as one might expect, that digital media was most effective in driving activity, like clicks and views, but that TV had a larger effect on brand perceptions. Other studies indicate that *Paid* media is most effective at driving traffic to the web and social media, while *Owned* media activity, like content on your website, increases social media awareness, which in turn increases likelihood to purchase and sales.

OPTIMIZATION

Load up on winners and cut back losers.

One of the other opportunities that having nearly real-time performance metrics from media gives us is the ability to adjust media campaigns on the fly. This is called *optimization*. The concept is fairly straight forwarded: take the current performance of different advertising vehicles, evaluate them in terms of your goals, then cut those that perform poorly and heavy up on those that are doing well; it's sort of like rebalancing your stock portfolio. Studying performance tells you not only which network or website to put your ads on, but also often what time period to use, what position to buy, and even which ad creative to run. The idea is to identify the best performing vehicle, context, and message, and then funnel your dollars there. This can, of course, get quite complex, and many a campaign is made or broken by how effectively optimization is managed.

It's impossible to fully know what's going to work until you try it.

The beginning part of any media campaign is the learning phase, where you actively test your best guesses, based on your strategic planning, for what the right advertising channels are and what the right messaging will be. In a perfect world, you will have conducted research before launching the campaign to make sure your choices are right, but it's almost never a perfect world.

Even with research, it's impossible to fully know what's going to work until you try it, so your campaign should plan to test alternative media and creative approaches right from the outset. This is often easier with media than with creative, since making multiple video commercials, for example, is often less financially feasible. As part of your buying process with media channels, you should negotiate complete flexibility, so you can quickly react to the data you see. Many platforms build in the capability for multi-variate testing, and the ability to make fast changes to media buys. This can make a big difference to the final performance of a campaign, so make sure that your team has a plan for optimization and testing for all your purchased advertising.

8. TRADITIONAL MEDIA

HANGIN' IN THERE?

TV and radio are evolving, but print is slipping.

Many of us grew up in a traditional advertising world. This has all changed as the digital sun has risen, but you'd be surprised by how many people still think it works the way it used to. As we all know digital has gobbled up so many things that were separate before: mail, TV, magazines, newspapers, books, music. For fun try making a list of how many things your smartphone can do that used to require a separate device.

The good news for the traditionalists among us is that old media is still alive and, if not full of vim and vinegar, at least not entirely decrepit. Broadcast media, TV and radio, have been going through their digital age challenges, with radio dealing with the internet and satellite, and TV up against time-shifting and streaming online. Both, however, have been holding their own despite the headwinds. That's because they are adapting. Media firm Carat projects that by 2020 80% of all media consumption globally will be digital. But TV viewing will actually go up, when you add digital TV channels to analog channels, and the same thing happens with radio and outdoor. The only one that seems to be in trouble is print, which keeps sliding.

Old media is still alive and, if not full of vim and vinegar, at least not entirely decrepit.

Radio is still a great tactical medium to reach someone in their car on the way to the store, as long as they are not listening to Spotify, and as we mentioned earlier, TV is effective for branding, if you can get by the fast-forward button. Outdoor has reinvented itself with digital signage, and even good old direct mail has value as an alternative to clogged up email boxes. In short, traditional media still has a valuable role to play. Not the same role as before, but as part of an overall system, old media can be an effective contributor.

As with all media choices, the channels you use should be those that your strategic planning told you were the most likely to influence your target consumer at that particular point in their journey. Taking those channels as a starting place, the next challenge is to understand the audience profile of the media vehicle and the context of the programming, to make sure it fits with your creative approach. Getting that alignment right drives the relevance and impact of your creative.

9. DIGITAL MEDIA

GROWING UP

Digital is projected to be over 50% of ad spending by 2020.

For years digital has been seeping into every nook and cranny of our lives (and with it digital advertising), but the shift of advertising money has been lagging behind the growth in digital usage. In a few years, however, most of the pundits project that digital ad spending will catch up and it will finish gobbling up most of the media world.

There are lots of kinds of digital ads, from banner ads and pop-up ads to video ads and native ads, which are ads masquerading as content. Almost every website that runs ads is part of an ad network. Some mobile apps also take advertising within their applications, as do games.

> **Valuable ways to expose your brand in the early stage of the consumer journey.**

Mobile is continuing to gather steam as we all spend more time on our smart devices and dollars flow in that direction. At the same time, location-specific advertising using a variety of technologies will increasingly connect with people at retail. Other digital advertising techniques that you may be familiar with, such as *Re-targeting*, serve ads to people who have already visited your website. These come later in the journey and are more often part of the cultivation process. *Geo-targeting*, *Contextual* and *Behavioral* ads, however, are relevant at this point in the journey because all three are valuable ways to expose your brand in the early stages.

GEO-TARGETING

> **Over half of mobile searches are looking for local results and most result in a purchase.**

People don't want advertising that interrupts what they are doing; they want companies that help them do it better. That's where geo-targeting and mobile can be so effective. *Geo-targeting* is where you can identify the user's city, ZIP Code, time zone, and more, using the IP address of their web connection, and, in turn, deliver smarter ads.

> **It can potentially deliver value when people want it most.**

Combined with mobile devices, it can potentially deliver value when people want it most. Brands like Quiznos and Denny's use it for coupons and special offers that you get when you are physically close. Local search already allows you to advertise to just the ZIP Codes around your stores: mobile geo-targeting lets you deliver ads as someone is driving by.

CONTEXTUAL

Contextual targeting of creative is the general trend across marketing.

The idea is that if an ad is related to the context that the viewer finds themselves in, it will be more relevant and thus more compelling. Contextual targeting can work for both branding and direct response campaigns by ensuring personal relevance. This only works, however, if the ad itself fits the context. That puts pressure on the brand to have creative variations designed to fit each context that the ad will run in; this contextual targeting of creative is the general trend across marketing.

Consumers tolerate ads styled like editorial if they are engaging.

Another style of ads is *Native ads*. These are advertising styled as editorial. While they create potential credibility problems for the integrity of the publisher, consumers don't seem to care too much, as long as they do not overtly sell too hard. The general acceptance of these types of ads seems to suggest that style is more important than substance for many consumers. It seems that as long as an ad is styled like an editorial and is entertaining or informative, they will tolerate it.

Digital ad networks also have the ability to automatically present ads to viewers that match the context. If you're on Yahoo and looking at content about smartphones, you then get ads related to smartphones. Although most contextual advertising in digital channels is automated, it can also be the result of smart human intervention, as with the brilliant Twitter ad that Oreo quickly put out in the Super Bowl when the stadium lights went out: "You can still dunk in the dark."

BEHAVIORAL

Tracking online behavior can improve response rates.

Online Behavioral Advertising, or OBA, is similar to contextual advertising in that it is targeting derived from inferring the user's interests and behaviors.

These inferences are based on information collected about the viewer's browsing behavior gathered with cookies (tiny programs that send information back to the host). Since ad networks have thousands of sites on their networks, behavioral advertising uses cookies and tracking pixels to follow a user from site to site, building a profile of the user and their interests. According to research from the Network Advertising Initiative, behavioral ads get clicks at a rate of 6.8% versus 2.8% for non-targeted ads. However, while studies show double the click rates for behavioral ads in some categories, in others it is far less effective. That's why, while a valuable part of your arsenal, OBA should be evaluated on a case-by-case basis.

In B2B, broadcast is not efficient, and print has been superseded by social media.

For most brands, especially in B2B, digital channels have become central to their efforts, and advertising on digital outlets is probably taking the majority of their media dollars. This makes sense for B2B, where broadcast is usually too broad, and where print has been superseded by digital trade press and industry social media. In B2C, while traditional media still can play an important role, budget pressures often push brands to a predominantly digital media strategy. And as digital videos have become more popular for presenting brand stories, rivaling the emotional impact of TV spots, this shift has accelerated.

Before we leave digital media, a word about email. Unsolicited email can be used for customer acquisition, but this kind of email has very poor response rates. While you don't hear quite so much about the spam tsunami these days, we are all still inundated with junk email. We are also better protected than ever by sophisticated spam filters. The bottom line is that acquisition email will get lost as part of the unsolicited daily wave of junk email, and will, at best, probably only get a response from active, ready-to-buy prospects. It's not impossible to use at this early point in the journey, but only if you have very highly qualified lists, which are very hard to come by and expensive, or an actively engaged prospect community and a product that doesn't require a great deal of pre-sell. Email becomes much more effective later as we consider how to cultivate prospects and strengthen customer relationships.

10. OWNED & EARNED MEDIA

DIRECT TO CONSUMER

Brands are shifting budgets from advertising to digital marketing.

Brand Advertising isn't the only way to introduce your company to new consumers. For many years the marketing world operated on a model where brands paid media companies to get their message out; the only way they could talk to their prospects was through third parties. But with the introduction of digital channels, brands found themselves with numerous new ways to connect directly with consumers without having to go through others. The result is that today brands can effectively use *Owned* and *Earned* media instead of *Paid* media. The advantages of this are numerous, not the least of which is that investments in Owned and Earned media often have long-term value versus the fleeting impact of advertising.

Investments in Owned and Earned media often have long-term value.

Brand Activation describes the Owned and Earned tactics that a brand can use to market itself to prospects and customers. It is yet another marketing buzz word, but it is useful. Brand Activation covers the spectrum of things that a brand can do to connect with a consumer other than advertising. Brand Activation is not to be confused with Demand Generation, another term that is commonly used, which refers specifically to producing leads, and comes later in the process.

Brand Activation includes:
- **Content marketing**—using content, in all its forms, to attract attention.
- **Influencer marketing**—leveraging influential people in social media.
- **Relationship marketing**—includes CRM, email, and loyalty programs.
- **Experiential marketing**—creating physical brand experiences.
- **Retail marketing**—display, POS, mobile, shopper marketing.
- **Promotion marketing**—designed to stimulate immediate sales or leads.

Of these, some lend themselves to this first step of introducing a brand to consumers, and some fit other stages of the journey better. For example, by the time the prospect gets to the store, you want them to already have a predisposition toward your brand, so *Retail* is not usually the best place to introduce new products and ideas. Similarly, *Promotion* marketing assumes that you've already created some value for your brand before putting it on sale. *Content, Influencer, Experiential* and *Relationship* marketing, are, however, all effective ways to introduce your brand to the world.

11. ACTIVATION CHANNELS

CONTENT MARKETING

The irony is that the more knowledge you give away, the more you'll sell.

Content is probably the most used word in marketing today. It means virtually anything you create to tell your story. Even ads are technically content. However, with consumer antipathy to ads, brands have pivoted to creating many other kinds of content to tell their story in a more engaging way. This ranges from videos to infographics, mobile apps, micro-sites, stunts, etc.

We will talk about content throughout this book because it infuses every aspect of modern marketing. At this initial stage of the game, however, content should be focused on attracting potential buyers with a very soft, preliminary engagement. At the beginning of the sales process, most people are not motivated to work hard studying and evaluating, and they don't like a hard sell. Instead they need to be enticed into engagement with the appropriate balance of entertainment and information. Clearly, some products and services lend themselves to being engaging more easily than others, and this is where creativity can solve the problem.

The strongest kind of content you can produce is content that people will want to share.

Perhaps the strongest kind of content you can produce is content that people will want to share in digital channels and that, as a result, will be highly ranked by the search engines. For example, fashion brand Nasty Gal's blog succeeds brilliantly in creating images of the cool life you too can live—if only you had the clothes. Great content, like theirs, combined with great SEO (search engine optimization) is extremely powerful, not only because it inspires your community to share it with friends, but also because it ensures that your content will appear, at no cost to you, in free organic search results. It's, therefore, a very smart investment as a way to attract new prospects.

INFLUENCER MARKETING

Social proof delivers powerful credibility.

One of the most profound changes that the digital age has enabled is the empowerment of word-of-mouth. It used to be that we could only tell our small circle of friends if we had a positive or negative experience with a brand. Now, through a multitude of platforms, every individual with a device has been given the power to express themselves and be heard by the entire world. People can post reviews of products and services, opinions of brands, likes, dislikes, and rants all over the web. In seconds, anyone can write a post, compose a review, snap a picture, shoot a video, even start a live stream, and be seen by hundreds, thousands or even millions of people. The average Facebook user has 155 friends, many have much more, and the viral power of their opinions only blossoms from there.

The opportunity is terrific to leverage happy consumers to spread their enthusiasm.

As a result, everyone has become an influencer and brands have to work hard to make us happy. Since there are no longer any places to hide poor products and bad service, inferior brand experiences of any sort get revealed very quickly and the damage can spread if it is not swiftly addressed. Conversely, the opportunity is terrific to leverage happy consumers to spread their enthusiasm. The Nielsen annual "Trust In Advertising" report consistently ranks recommendations from friends as the most trusted source of information. Recommendations create awareness with new prospects and introduce the brand to others with more credibility than advertising ever can.

Although we're all influencers, there are also super influencers, who can be very valuable. In this media-saturated world, curators and tastemakers matter because they help us get to what's good faster. This has given rise to super influencers, who include all the celebrities who tweet, as well as people with loyal followings, who sell access to their followers in a variety of ways. This might be ads on their websites, native ads disguised as editorial, or even their outright endorsement. Kate Arends, for example, has a beauty and fashion following of 2.6 million people, and she posts products she recommends to her Pinterest board.

While super influencers can be enlisted to help at a cost, consumers are accustomed now to sharing their own thoughts and opinions, and there are many things that a brand can do to make this easier for them. If you take your family on the Buzz Lightyear ride at Disney world, for example, they snap a picture mid-ride and send it to you. The first thing you do is share it on Facebook and Disney gets all that exposure for nothing. This is low-hanging fruit for most brands, delivers terrific returns for the small investment required, and should be one of the first things you do in the hunt to introduce your story to new prospects.

RELATIONSHIP MARKETING

Happy customers tell their friends, who tell their friends; and so the ripples flow.

Closely related to Influencer marketing is Relationship marketing. In our CRM world (customer relationship marketing) customers and prospects become valuable relationships that your brand must keep and invest in. The basic objective is to create loyal customers and grow their lifetime value. But one of the big side benefits of having an enthusiastic community of fans, is that those customers will go out into the world and spread the word to their networks. The objective is, therefore, to identify, inspire and equip your most loyal customers to say good things about your brand to their friends on social networks. This includes Ratings & Reviews and social posts.

When you buy a car today, the ink is barely dry when the dealer asks you to post a review. They make it very easy, send you a special link, give you an easy rating and review tool, and even outright beg for a good review. Part of their sales process is to leverage your happiness with your new car while you are still enjoying the glow of the moment.

Identify, inspire and equip your most loyal customers to say good things about your brand.

This is only one way to activate your happy customers. There are many others that you can use once you have a database. Building a database takes time, but when you have it, it's worth its weight in gold. Working with Royal Caribbean Cruises, we quickly discovered their secret weapon was their multi-million strong database of past and current customers. From this database they would not only fill empty berths at the last minute, but also refresh their network of prospects.

Another important piece, even at this early stage of the game, is customer service. While every company tries to be perfect, as long as people are imperfect there will be problems. Customer service has always been the way to address these challenges, but now it has become even more important with social media. This has created the opportunity for brands to very publicly demonstrate the proof of their values, how much they care and how they keep their Brand Promises. When a kid left his stuffed giraffe "Joshie" at the Ritz Carlton, the hotel not only found it, but concocted a series of photos of "Joshie" lounging by the pool, watching TV and even getting a massage. The cute photos spread quickly around social media highlighting the extra effort the Ritz Carlton makes to keep even stuffed guests happy. More common examples are the fast response by customer service to complaints online. These moments are very visible opportunities for the brand to quickly solve issues and create fans. Amplified by social media, it's always a powerful opportunity to show how much a brand cares.

PR, which is the traditional form of influencer marketing, may be relevant early in the game too—but only if you have something of note to share. To paraphrase Seth Godin, if you want to be remarked upon, be remarkable. The dynamics are a little different than with customer word-of-mouth. Press and bloggers usually require stories that are newsworthy, which often creates a higher bar than brands may be able to reach in the normal course of business.

EXPERIENTIAL MARKETING

People seem to enjoy real-world experience even more.

Creating brand experiences in the real world is becoming more common as consumers seem to relish the opportunity to interact in the flesh. Perhaps because we live so much of lives in our little digital bubbles, people seem to enjoy real-world experiences even more. This is one reason why many retailers are incorporating unique experiential environments in stores, and why many brands are turning to experiential marketing to get awareness and trial at the grass roots level. Experiential marketing is distinct from Retail marketing in that it's about the event or experience instead of where it's located. Events can introduce a brand or reinforce its story. Lean Cuisine, for example, invited women to "weigh in" with a selection of special scales in New York's Grand Central Station. The scales let the women decide how they really wanted to be "weighed." Instead of pounds, they could opt for education, the number of people they help, or just being good mothers. The experience created credibility, content, and sharing that no ad could achieve.

Brands are turning to experiential marketing for awareness and trial.

Experiential marketing also includes sponsorships and sampling, both of which can be leveraged to introduce people to your brand. High awareness sponsorship events that fit the brand can be used to enhance reputation, as well as social media awareness, and sampling at events is a time-tested way to get your product into lots of hands.

12. CREATIVE

MADE YOU LOOK

Compelling, original creativity is always a competitive advantage.

The general acceptance of these types of ads seems to suggest that style is more important than substance for many consumers. It seems that as long as an ad is styled like an editorial and is entertaining or informative, they will tolerate it. This would be reflected in things like logo design, the brand style guide and the general Voice and Tone parameters that you set for how your brand is presented. Creativity becomes even more important as you reach out to introduce your brand to consumers for the first time. Translating your Brand Identity, and all of the ideas that ladder up to it, into advertising and activation is the work of your creative team, either within your own organization or at your agency.

What really counts is if the work delivers the desired results.

Contrary to some would-be artists who end up in advertising, creativity's only purpose in marketing is to assist in achieving business goals. That's why while all the creativity awards in the world might be great, what really counts is if the work delivers the desired results. Though the mission of the creativity within an ad or piece of content might change as tactics change, a few things are common creative challenges for most everything you do in Brand Advertising and Brand Activation.

In a world that's so full of images, messages and interruptions designed to steal our attention, the first challenge is to get that attention. Imagine what might make you actually look at something instead of glazing over and moving on. It certainly isn't the same thing you've seen before. It's invariably something unusual or surprising. Or it might be something you have seen a thousand times, but presented from a different perspective, so you look with fresh eyes. When GE wanted to show that it's new Café Refrigerator could serve up hot water too, the print ad featured an ice-bound penguin breathing fire. Other examples of made-you-look marketing are no further than the bottom of your average webpage. Those clickbait ads combine a provocative picture with a headline tease to make us pay attention and sometimes even click.

Keeping someone's attention is a great deal harder than getting it.

Keeping someone's attention, however, is a great deal harder than getting it. But if you're successful, you get a chance to tell your story. At this early stage when introducing your brand, it's critical to remember that your audience is delicate, and the slightest push too hard can cause them to fly away. Instead, you need to entice audiences into your story. Whether it's a web page, or a TV spot, or a video online, it must get the balance between engagement and information just right.

INCREMENTAL ENGAGEMENT

The cumulative effect of the journey creates the preference you seek.

Keep in mind that the vast majority of consumers are far from ready to buy during the early stages. But the temptation is often to let the priorities of the business push you toward a heavier sell than is appropriate for the moment. That's why consumers need to be led, gently, toward brand awareness and preference. This is only the first of many steps that they will take as they form their opinion of your brand and move towards a purchase, so you have to be patient. It's part of a process of *Incremental Engagement*, which recognizes that each touch adds a layer of understanding, and the cumulative effect of the journey creates the preference you seek.

Think of each ad or piece of content as a brick in the brand house.

Don't fall prey to the temptation to pour your entire value proposition into every piece of creative. Instead, think of each ad or piece of content as a brick in the brand house you are building. According to research by AdEspresso, the more an ad is seen, the less effective it becomes as ad fatigue sets in. This means your prospects will need to see a constant stream of new messages from you over time. Imagine it like a courtship: patiently build a generous, valuable relationship, and love will not be far behind.

SWING FOR THE FENCES

Don't be afraid of big ideas.

Originality in how you tell your brand story will always have great power. But great creative is hard to legislate. When it happens, it feels like magic, and its effect on the success of a brand can be enormous. Old Spice was a tired, old brand—something your grandfather used. But its re-introduction made it cool again, almost purely with creativity. The "Smell like a man, man" campaign with Mustafa started in 2010 and took off with online video. It understood its audience of young men and how to speak to them. It was funny, irreverent, and spread like wildfire, demonstrating that a good idea is just as powerful as a whole lot of media money.

Trust the skills of your creative team and your intuition.

In today's social media-powered culture, brands like Old Spice can win consumer hearts through great creative, without needing to spend enormous amounts on media. This should inspire all brands to take creative and branding risks and invest more in original content because even getting close to a hit can catapult a brand faster than almost anything else. Since digital released the audience from its captivity, big creative ideas have become even more powerful. But they are scary. They feel risky because no one has done them before, which is precisely their power. One way to think of the power of creative is in terms of impact. A strong ad needs to be seen far fewer times than a weak ad, before it works. That means you don't have to spend as much on media. It comes down to a risk/reward calculation, which is difficult with creative.

This is not the nuts-and-bolts part of business, and it's understandably difficult for an executive in, perhaps, a risk-averse environment, to take an uncertain leap of faith. When Wendy's went after their competitors with "Where's the Beef?" or Dove threw out the airbrushed beauty standards and got real, or someone at Absolut decided to invest in crazy bottle photography, there was little evidence to support their decision. All the strategy and brand work they had done took them to a moment when someone had to trust their intuition, trust the vision of their creative team, and take a risk. However, as we end this discussion of creativity, it must be said that for most companies and brands the immediate opportunity is not to create the extraordinary campaign, but to put the nuts and bolts of a modern marketing system in place.

CHAPTER 4

COURTING SUCCESS

Cultivating prospects until they are ready to become buyers

EXECUTIVE SUMMARY

You've studied your target consumers, refined your brand and created awareness with your audience. But most of these prospects are not ready to buy. You, therefore, need to cultivate and nurture them until the magic moment arrives.

Mass Selling

- The internet is the first medium that can simulate a salesperson.
- The vast majority of consumers are not ready to buy.
- Most consumers need to be cultivated before they buy.
- Much of selling is being in the right place at the right time, so just stay connected.
- Technology gives brands the data they need to automate much of the personalized selling process that was previously handled by sales people.

Earning Trust

- Consumers don't want to be sold; they want to be in control. Don't force them to talk to a salesperson just because you think it gives you an advantage. It doesn't. They are more likely to just go somewhere else.
- Consumers want to make the best choices. They also want the process to be easy and enjoyable.
- Brands can earn trust by providing answers and making the process easy. But do not attempt to manipulate the consumer. They will see it and punish your brand.

Delivering Value

- Content is the currency of cultivation. Brands exchange content for the consumer's time and attention.
- The more relevant and compelling your content is, the more valuable the consumer will find it.
- Give away your knowledge. It will attract buyers, build trust and result in leads.
- Cultivating is not selling, it is creating the conditions for preference to form.
- Make sure your content has real value and integrity for the consumer.

The Hard Stuff

- The hardest thing for brands is to create a continuous flow of high-quality content.
- Effective content doesn't need to be expensive, just engaging and relevant.
- Great content requires strong strategic guidance.
- The secret of great content is a great content team.

Build a System

- Marketing technology makes mass automated cultivation possible.
- Before you can deliver personalized content at the right time to the right person, you need to put your systems in place.
- Marketing technology such as marketing automation (MAP), customer relationship management (CRM), and content management systems (CMS) are readily available and accessible to even small companies.

Tactics

- Inbound tactics attract consumers to your Owned media such as your website. For example, content with search engine optimization (SEO) will attract searchers.
- Outbound tactics include activity triggered email, retargeting, drip marketing lifecycle campaigns, text, mobile apps, and more.
- Permission mail is still the unsung hero of marketing.

Be Useful

- Consumers don't want an annuity, they want a stable retirement; they don't want a weed killer, they want a beautiful yard. Brands that help consumers achieve their goals earn their trust, loyalty, and business.

- Find ways to be useful to your consumers, and they will stay connected to you.

---

1. SELLING IN THE DIGITAL AGE

CONSULTATIVE SELLING

Mass one-to-one selling is now possible.

Many people feel they understand sales but feel much less clear about marketing. The dynamics are, however, very similar and the goal is exactly the same: persuade your prospects that your product or service is the one they should want. Consider how a good salesperson sells. When you walk into an auto showroom the first thing a salesperson will do is to engage you. He or she will be pleasant and start earning the likeability and relationship that leads to trust. In those moments, the salesperson is communicating a great deal in how he conducts himself. He will quickly start to ask you questions. Are you interested in a car or a truck? Is this for you or for a family member? For business or for pleasure? This is the essential sales process of discovering what is relevant to the prospect. It's critically important, because if someone wants a truck and a salesperson starts talking about cars, the prospect will quickly lose interest. As the salesperson gathers information, he constantly tailors and tweaks his pitch, getting increasingly personally relevant. This is called consultative selling.

The internet is the first marketing medium that can simulate the consultative selling of a salesperson.

Until the internet came along the only consultative selling came from a salesperson. Marketing couldn't do it because traditional media was one-way. Marketing could talk at you but couldn't listen to you. The internet changed that with a medium that could enable a real-time exchange of information. The result was marketing that could simulate a consultative selling process. This really came to life with high-speed broadband, which enabled almost instantaneous communications. It was the first time marketing could, in essence, act like a good salesperson. This extraordinary capability is sometimes lost today among all the other amazing things that the internet can do. But this ability to act like a salesperson has changed both sales and marketing forever. Now when we talk about cultivation, we are talking about mass consultative selling on steroids.

LEAD NURTURING

The vast majority of leads never convert because of poor lead nurturing.

As we know, most people are not ready to buy when a brand connects with them for the first time. In the previous chapter, we discussed how to make that initial connection. We outlined how to use Brand Advertising and Brand Activation to introduce your brand, and why, instead of just focusing on the tiny percentage of prospects who might be ready to buy at that moment, you should also target the entire audience with a cultivation program.

The idea is to turn a first contact into an on-going dialogue in which you cultivate and nurture a lead's interest until they are ready to buy.

On the surface, cultivation for most brands means a process of incrementally presenting your value proposition, your pitch, until the prospect has heard your whole story, and hopefully found it persuasive. It assumes that you are confident that when you have the chance to tell your complete story, you will get the desired result. Telling your story might be pretty quick and easy if it's about bubble gum, but explaining something more complicated, such as where to invest your retirement savings, is neither quick nor easy. Many brands have complex value propositions, which take time and effort to explain and understand. And even simple brands, with simple value propositions, frequently need time with their prospects to win them over.

Either way, the problem is often just getting enough of your prospect's time and attention so you can tell your story. Conventional wisdom holds that it takes 7–13 touches to get your value proposition across. This is complicated by what appears to be a lengthening sales cycle for many brands. Those with considered purchases or complex products, especially in B2B, have already notoriously long sales cycles that are just getting longer.

In a face-to-face selling situation, you might be able to get all the time you need in one meeting, but with most marketing interactions, you usually only have time to communicate a piece of the story. That forces brands to think about the order in which they present their value proposition, literally, the stages of the pitch, as well as the cumulative effect of different messages layering on top of one another over time. This is the essence of the lead-nurturing process, the design of which should also reflect a comprehensive understanding of the psychology of your target consumer, as we outlined in Chapter 2.

CONSIDERATION & EVALUATION

Companies that are good at lead nurturing get more sales at less cost.

The cultivation process happens during the *Consideration* and *Evaluation* phases of the consumer journey.

The stages of the consumer journey:

1. **Trigger** — What causes a consumer to begin thinking about a purchase?
2. **Consideration** — Is this purchase necessary and feasible? What will it mean?
3. **Evaluation** — Which product is better and why?
4. **Purchase** — How and where is the purchase made? Why should you buy now? Is it easy?
5. **Loyalty** — What is the experience of the product? Will customers become advocates?

You've already got your prospect's attention in some way with your initial marketing trigger; now, what do you do with it? The old way was to immediately try to close the deal, and if prospects were not ready to buy that was their problem. The new way is to engage, find out what's important, and nurture that interest up to the point where they value your brand and are ready to buy. This includes prospects not fully sold yet, people with unaddressed objections, people still actively evaluating their options, and the just curious.

A good deal of lead nurturing is just managing to stay connected and top-of-mind until the right moment comes.

It also includes the many prospects who may already be sold on your brand, but for whom the timing is just not right yet. Bad timing can be for a million reasons that have nothing to do with your brand. But if you stay connected, as good salespeople know, the time will often come when these prospects are ready to buy. Then you'll be there, connected, pre-sold, and ready to close.

2. LEAD IDENTIFICATION

REMOVING BARRIERS

The internet is your new sales team.

At the start of the process, your prospects may see a number of ads or pieces of content before they take an action. What brands traditionally want prospects to do is raise their hands, identify themselves and say, "I'm a prospect, here I am, come and sell me." Before the internet came along raising your hand was about all consumers could do if they wanted to learn more, even with the knowledge that by identifying themselves they were inviting the often unwelcome attentions of a salesperson. But that was then, when salespeople were about the only way to find out more.

Today, consumers expect they can do all the research they need online without having to deal with a salesperson until they are ready. Strangely, however, many companies and industries don't get this. They have always required consumers to talk to their sales people from the beginning of the process, and they have difficulty letting go of this idea. This, despite the reality that in most situations consumers today want to be left alone until they decide they are ready to connect. In cars sales, for example, consumers aren't waiting for dealers to change and are already jumping on new types of sellers, like Carvana.com, which let you buy a car without ever talking to a salesperson.

In financial services, a category our agency has worked in for years, the sales model is often built around the financial advisor. Since early in the last century, financial advisors have been the sales force for their industry. That's because industry wisdom has always held that consumers are incapable of understanding financial offerings without the guidance of a friendly expert. Except when they are not, which is increasingly the case. A study from Ispos and LinkedIn showed that only 5% of millennials intend to rely on a financial advisor and 91% said they intend to use their social networks for advice. Despite this, many traditional financial services companies cling to the old ways. This is even in the face of challenges from numerous new financial start-ups, such as Wealthfront and Betterment, which are focused on empowering people with knowledge, insights, and control: just what people are looking for.

> Companies still make access to knowledge difficult for consumers in the belief that it will force them to talk to their salespeople.

What restricting access to knowledge actually does is force prospects to find other companies that will not make them jump through hoops. The mindset that underlies this attempt to control people is the byproduct of the age when companies were actually able to successfully manipulate consumers. The reality of our world today, however, is that any attempt to do anything but serve the interests of the consumer, will backfire and produce exactly the opposite of what was intended.

PERSONALIZED RELEVANCE

> Individually relevant content and communication is now a basic expectation.

Removing barriers and making customer experiences easy doesn't mean that brands have to be less persuasive. Instead the focus should be on how personally relevant the lead nurturing experience can be. This is shaped by a combination of data, consumer insights and user experience design. Data from digital interactions can tell you which website a lead comes from, where they're located, or even what company they work for. If they are already a customer, you might also know their purchase history, what content they have seen or shared on your sites, and what ratings and reviews they may have given you.

The more individually relevant a value proposition is, the more compelling it will be.

All of this is grist for the personalization mill, which, when combined with your understanding of your prospect persona's buying behavior, will allow you to plan in advance the most effective, step-by-step presentation of your value proposition for each of your target personas. The idea is to take the Consumer Journey Mapping, Personas, Content Strategy and Messaging Frameworks that you developed in your strategic planning and use that knowledge to design content and messaging for each step of the journey for each target persona. Then, using behavioral data to identify the persona of a prospect, you can deliver exactly the right, personally relevant content for that persona at the right moment. This systematic approach is the equivalent of a sales person listening and saying exactly the right thing at each stage of a consultative pitch. It's a process that can turn prospects into new customers, new customers into loyal customers and loyal customers into brand ambassadors. It's also how marketing can amplify and empower sales without the need for more sales reps.

3. THE ROLE OF CONTENT

SETTING THE TABLE

Content creates the conditions in which the prospect wants to buy.

Your cultivation system is the equivalent of a whole new sales force. Once it is up and running, it can identify enough about prospects that it will give you the chance to say the right thing to each of them at the right time. What you say at each one of those moments will be in the form of some kind of content. By now, you are probably sick of reading about content. It has become one of those marketing buzzwords that is so overused it might even be damaging the credibility of the concept. Nevertheless, with the content possibilities unleashed by the web and technology, content has become even more important in marketing than before.

The trick is to make engaging content that serves your marketing and sales purposes, but does not appear to be selling.

The shift to a focus on content in marketing has mirrored the shift of power from companies to consumers. With consumers in charge, brands have no choice but to cater to their needs and wants. And they have told us very clearly that they want more content versus advertising. Since we are all experienced consumers, we can fairly easily tell the difference between the two. Advertising is trying to sell us something; It's pushing us to buy and assumes we care about its pitch. It's an interruption that we don't want most of the time. Content, on the other hand, is something that we do want. It's engaging, entertaining, informative and even useful. It's something we seek out because of an interest, something that helps us make choices, and something that we might even want to share. The trick for brands is to make content that does not appear to be selling but serves your marketing and sales purposes. This, as the best sales people will tell you, is classic consultative selling, which instead of selling, creates the conditions in which the prospect wants to buy.

COMPETITION FOR ATTENTION

Consumers are short-attention-span skimmers.

With the growth of digital channels, broadband and portable devices, consumers can easily get enormous amounts of content anywhere, anytime. This is something relatively new, and it's producing an explosion of content creation, from millions of videos on YouTube to a new golden age of TV on Hulu, Netflix, and a host of other websites and networks. Add to that 24/7 sports for almost any interest, a non-stop news cycle from hundreds of sources, and do-it-yourself streaming video, and you've just scratched the surface. It's the most compelling and competitive content environment imaginable. And it's into this fierce arena that you submit your content in the hope that consumers will choose to spend their time with it versus all the other choices they have.

There have never been more content choices of higher quality fighting for people's time and attention.

While this general content landscape is brutally competitive, it is possible, however, for brand content, if constructed with the right elements, to break through the noise. On the plus side is the changing nature of content consumption itself. On mobile devices, for example, people prefer short videos. Mobile on tablets or smartphones is a lean-forward experience and feeds consumer's developing desire to be constantly stimulated. For better or for worse, consumers are short-attention-span skimmers, looking for instant gratification, fast answers and continuous engagement. While the average length of video viewed varies depending on the channel, the overall average length of a video online comes in at about 30 seconds. This burgeoning demand actually aligns nicely with brands which need to keep themselves in front of content-hungry consumers.

4. CONTENT STRUCTURE

MAKING IT EASY

Getting to clear-cut answers quickly is usually harder than most people expect.

Helping to make content marketing work is the consumer desire to be in charge of their own research and evaluation. Or at least to feel like they are. Consumers have an expectation that they can make smart, informed decisions by researching virtually anything with the internet. The reality, as we've mentioned before, is that getting to clear-cut answers quickly and easily is usually harder than most people want or expect. This is where many brands have successfully inserted themselves as trusted guides for their audiences. The annual Trust in Advertising Study from A.C. Nielsen continues to show brand websites being second only to "recommendations from a friend" in trustworthiness. This is terrific news for brands as it reveals that consumers really value and trust brand websites, which just happen to be the place where brands have the best opportunity to tell their story. Brands are winning this stellar endorsement from consumers because they are delivering on the promise of search for their consumers. They are doing this by delivering content that lets consumers feel like they are fully informed. This is an opportunity for your company to figure out what consumers want to know about your category, give it to them, and earn their trust in return.

> **Consumers want to do their own research and make the best choices, but only if it's easy and the content is reliable.**

Underlying a successful cultivation effort are the Content Strategy and Messaging Frameworks that we discussed in Chapter 1. These specify what each piece of content needs to say and how it needs to be said. They become the guides that marketers and creatives follow, informed by the brand's Personality and Identity, as discussed in Chapter 2. Together these inputs determine the right balance, for each target persona, of analytical and emotional elements in any content you create.

MAKING IT FUN

> **People want to feel emotionally connected to their brands.**

On the analytical side of the equation, consumers want to know the facts about a brand and its category so they can make smart, informed choices. They want to know the good and the bad and have confidence that what they are being told is true and reliable. Underlying this is an expectation that they can find out everything they need to know from search and brand websites, and a willingness to give brands their trust, unless they have a reason not to. Imagine what a complicated world it would be if you did not trust anyone or anything. Consumers feel the same way. Life is complicated and busy. They have a great deal to do and not enough time to do it, so they will trust a brand as long as it remains trustworthy. On the other hand, woe be to the brand that is caught manipulating the truth. The Volkswagen debacle, where they faked test results, destroyed decades of trust and damaged the integrity of an entire industry. Imagine how they will repair that trust, which is table-stakes in all commercial relationships today.

On the emotional side, consumers want the process of getting to their goal of picking the best product to be not only quick and easy, but also fun and engaging. This is especially true early in their journey when they are less motivated to expend effort, and when content can bring the Brand Personality and Identity to life. The old adage "Love the ad, love the product," rings true at this point in the journey because people want to feel emotionally connected to their brands, even B2B brands can be loved, although that often translates as trust.

In many categories, the emotional side of the brand is actually much more powerful than the analytical side.

It's no surprise that our emotions are often stronger than our cool, analytical side. The same is true for how we react to the different sides of a brand story. The mix is often determined by the nature of the brand itself. A brand might need to lean on the emotional side more because of a very simple value proposition, as in chewing gum or soda, or because it's driven by lifestyle associations, as in fashion. In every situation, there is a mix of hard and soft attributes, where hard attributes are facts, features and benefits, and soft attributes are emotional associations. Every brand needs to find its place on the continuum, with hard attributes on one end and soft at the other. Your work with strategic planning in Chapter 1 will have revealed the right balance for your brand.

5. THOUGHT LEADERSHIP

GIVING IT AWAY

Your mission is not just to sell your products, but to help your customers.

Some brands have very entertainment-oriented content strategies designed for emotional engagement. They often do this because their product category does not, in itself, get the audience very excited. Insurance is one of those not-very-exciting categories. That's why the mission of our agency's videos for GEICO was solely to engage the audience. Short, funny videos were created to engage the audience sufficiently to create awareness for the brand's simple message "15 minutes could save you 15% on car insurance." This works for GEICO because their value proposition is very uncomplicated, and the biggest challenge they face is just to get people to pay attention to it. Other brands, where their value proposition is complex and requires study, often can't get away with an entertainment first approach, and often need to take a step-by-step, thought-leadership approach. This is especially true in B2B.

When we first started working with IBM they had just acquired the business consulting arm of PwC. A couple of years later they sold their computer manufacturing business to Lenovo in China. This was part of a shift from being a product-oriented company to a customer-oriented company. The thinking behind the moves was simply that computer products were becoming commodities, and that they were really in the business of making businesses successful, hence the consulting company acquisition. It also triggered a shift to leading with thought leadership, which we were fortunate enough to be part of. The idea was simple:

> **Give the knowledge away and you will get brand preference and leads in return.**

IBM began to share what they knew as a way to help customers and prospects understand and solve problems. As a result, they continued to grow as a trusted knowledge source, a go-to provider of information and insights. Not far behind came engagement and sales. We saw this open, generous approach work, just as the open-source movement worked. It was the reflection of a new contract between companies and their consumers, where their mission was not to just to sell their products, but to help their customers.

CONTENT INTEGRITY

> **Respect your consumers. They're smarter than you think.**

Underlying a successful thought-leadership strategy has to be a commitment to the integrity and value of the content itself. Consumers are not stupid and will see through a manipulation. Content has to be genuinely designed to serve the needs of the consumer first. If it does that well, then there is a tacit understanding that it may bring with it the opportunity for the brand to engage. This is the new marketing contract. Just like we were all willing to sit through commercials to watch a TV show, or ads to get to the next article, we're willing to give our time and attention to a brand, if it can earn it. But it's not enough to just have appropriate content for each engagement; content needs to be better if a brand wants to stand out. Odds are your competitors have figured out that content is important too. So, assuming everyone is pursuing the same ends, the brand with the most engaging content and the clearest commitment to their consumers, wins.

Thought leadership content that is a thinly veiled sales pitch will be quickly seen for what it is and damage the brand.

A big part of that commitment is transparency and openness. In this social world, consumers are very attuned to the reputational honesty of brands. It's very hard for a brand to ask to be a trusted knowledge source, while being seen to be less than honest in other areas. This means brands have to be alert to how they are perceived from all sides, so that everything they do supports their integrity. This is bigger than just the sales process, and it reflects the need for companies to truly live their values and protect their reputation at all costs.

SEO AFTERBURNERS

Sidestep the need to pay third parties to deliver your messages.

You can create a piece of content, put it on your website, and it can travel out to the four corners of the web, connecting with prospects at exactly the moment they are looking for it. Imagine if you are wondering how to sell those hand-carved chess pieces you made, and all of a sudden twenty people call you looking for hand-carved chess pieces. Content combined with search is no less magical.

The remarkable thing about content is that it can attract exactly the people it is designed for.

Maximizing the potential for this is SEO, or search engine optimization. It is one part science and two parts art. Your content needs to be designed so that it is highly desirable by consumers, as defined by the search engines, and you need to ensure that it is tagged and positioned in exactly the right way. The opportunities for brands, which get this formula right, are significant because they can sidestep the need to pay third parties to deliver their messages and replace paid ads with free exposure. The challenge is that you cannot buy this exposure; you have to earn it.

6. CONTENT CREATION

EXCELLENCE IN EXECUTION

Brands are producing lots of content and the bar keeps rising.

Since the proliferation of high-speed broadband, especially on mobile, consumer preference for video content has skyrocketed. According to Cisco, 85% of internet traffic will be video by 2019. This has put even more pressure on brands to create video content that not only supports the cultivation process, but also rises above the undifferentiated noise. All brand content, however, doesn't have to be an Academy Award winner. But it does have to be relevant, engaging, and reflective of your Brand Identity. This is hard in the best of circumstances, but it is even harder when you have to produce a continuous flow of content week in and week out. While your cultivation process for prospects may be fed by a library of fairly evergreen content, your customers, and perhaps many of your prospects, will still need fresh content, delivered continuously, to stay engaged with your brand until they are ready to buy.

Modern marketing requires that companies produce and distribute engaging content all the time in order to stay top-of-mind.

You may burn through all your evergreen, value proposition content with a prospect and still not close the deal because the timing is just not right. That leaves you with the task of staying connected with that person in whom you have invested so much time, effort ,and content, until they become ready, relying less on selling and more on engagement to keep the connection alive. The challenge is to produce a constant flow of content that will ensure you don't lose your connection.

THE RIGHT TEAM

Experienced, talented writers, designers, and producers are in short supply.

One reason companies find content so hard to make is that it is usually a very different discipline from what they do every day. Manufacturing and distributing products, or being a retailer, is a completely different world, and set of skills, from making videos, writing thought leadership articles, creating compelling blog posts, or producing engaging podcasts. Some brands set up an in-house team to do this, others work with an agency. Either can be effective if you have a team blessed with the experience and talents for this kind of work.

Great content is often as much about the experience and abilities of the team as the amount of money that is spent.

The challenge is to consistently produce original, engaging content over time. This doesn't mean it needs to be expensive, because sometimes a simple approach works just as well. But it does mean that the strategic underpinnings, creative sensibilities, and originality of the work must be of the highest order. If your content is the same as everything else out there, it will be less likely to be, viewed, shared, or create brand preference. In an environment with thousands of companies producing enormous amounts of bland, undifferentiated content, it really doesn't make sense to enter this contest unless you commit to do what's necessary to win.

The difficulty with having an in-house team is finding and keeping the right people. With the growth of content production, experienced, talented writers, designers, and producers are in short supply. Conversely, working with agencies can be a slow and expensive business. Many agencies still don't understand that producing content for digital channels is not the same as producing big-budget TV commercials. The challenge is to produce an on-going stream of quality content that can engage prospects for a workable budget. If you have to produce a video every week, the cost structure and production approach has to be appropriate. Companies must get this piece of the puzzle right, because content is the last mile—the final connection point. Its impact will determine if all your work to put the right message in front of your target consumer, at the right time, is successful or for naught.

7. THE CULTIVATION SYSTEM

THE BIG PICTURE

Marketing without data is like flying in a storm without instruments.

The idea is to create a system that automates the delivery of content to the right person at the right time. While some of this happens in Paid and Earned media channels, it is particularly critical this you get this right in your Owned channels, because that's where you can have the biggest impact during the evaluation process. There are many moving pieces in the nurturing process, so it's helpful to see the big picture.

The Cultivation System:

Objective:
Automate the process of nurturing leads and moving customers to conversion and beyond to loyalty and advocacy

Method:
Use strategic planning outputs to determine the right content and messaging for each persona at each interaction point in their journey.

Use CRM and MAP data to identify the persona of new leads or customers.

Deliver appropriate content for the persona and activity trigger.

Every time you connect with consumers, but do not immediately turn them into a sale, you move into cultivation mode. The strategy is to figure out as much about them as possible, even though they might be anonymous, and then to tailor a step-by-step process of engagement, education, and persuasion, using content tailored to their persona, behavior, and stage of the journey.

The inherent two-way nature of the internet combined with marketing software like CRM, MAP, and CMS have made it possible for companies to automate the cultivation and lead nurturing process, much of which used to be handled by sales, if at all. This enables mass, personalized, consultative selling for the first time.

Before you can automate a cultivation system you will need to have the right technology infrastructure in place.

For this system to work, you are going to need some or all of the software we mentioned above and perhaps a few other pieces of technology. The good news is that this marketing system infrastructure is quite mature and accessible for most companies. We will go into it in more depth in Chapter 7, when we discuss constructing the system.

KNOWN VS. ANONYMOUS

If you just focus on your customers, you won't mess up too badly.

Assuming you already have those infrastructure pieces in place, in practical terms there are two ways to get the system started. First, and most effective, is to get prospects to give you their email address. MAP such as HubSpot or Pardot, let you associate activity with that person. That means, for example, if they come to your website and look at a specific product, say a premium lawnmower, you will know who it is. This identification is accomplished by tying someone's email address to the anonymous IP address that is available for every digital visitor to your site. Knowing who they are and what they have looked at in the past will let you tailor what they see on your website every time they visit. Having their email address will also let you keep the process alive by reaching out with emails that continue the conversation, such as providing advice about lawn maintenance.

With an email address in hand your software can associate viewing activity on your Owned media with that person.

Alternatively, if you don't get an email address, because many consumers are wary of giving it out, you can use their IP address to automatically tailor their experience based on the activity you have observed for that IP previously. This will let you present increasingly relevant content experiences to anonymous visitors on your website, but it will not let you proactively reach out using email. While not as good as having the email address, just having the IP identification lets you recognize when someone comes back to your site. That way, the content you offer can be targeted to them based on what they have viewed in the past. This is not perfect, but it supports the cultivation process, albeit anonymously.

In an ideal world, you would skim off the 1%–2% of ready-to-buy people immediately, then capture the email addresses of the remaining 98% and cultivate them until one by one they all become buyers. Not being an ideal world, of course, the battle is not only to close deals with those ready to buy, but to convert as many as possible of the rest into your cultivation program.

8. NURTURING TACTICS

INBOUND

It's better if you get an email address, but it's ok if you don't.

In addition to figuring out what content you will need for each situation, your strategic planning will also tell you what cultivation tactics to use, when and for which personas. These include both inbound tactics, where prospects come to you, and outbound tactics, where you reach out to them. The idea of inbound marketing is to attract prospects to your Owned media, such as your website or your social sites, and for the majority who do not immediately convert, then begin the lead nurturing process in as personalized a way as possible. They can come to your website from numerous places, such as from a banner ad, a social post, a third-party site, or from search. In each instance, you will often know where the visitor comes from, and based on that, you can infer some information. This will allow you to tailor the landing page that they see when they arrive so that it aligns with what you know about them.

The objective is to present the visitor with the most relevant information and experience for who they are, and where they are on their consumer journey.

Landing pages are custom pages within your website. They can be designed to be everything from a customized home page to a simple promotional page. Most Content Management Systems (CMS), which are designed to manage the content on websites, require that you create a unique landing page for each situation, but increasingly the next generation of CMS software, such as Sitecore or the Adobe suite, use a *Smart Content* approach. This automatically re-organizes the layout of a homepage based on profile data, so that it is tailored with just the right content and messaging for the viewer who has been identified.

Marketing Automation Platforms (MAP) will identify when a visitor returns and will tell you if their IP address has appeared on your social sites. If, however, more than one person is using the same IP address, as with company's web addresses, you will not be able to differentiate between individual viewers. However, if you have their email address, which, as we discussed, should be a key objective, you will be able to track them as an individual and know if they respond to any of your outbound efforts.

All this might make your eyes glaze over, but your takeaway should be that your team can now easily create a truly personalized experience for leads and customers. These capabilities are being rapidly adopted by companies large and small. Marketing automation, the newest marketing technology, was already in about 60% of companies over $500 million and in 10% of companies $20–$500 million in 2014 according to Raab Associates. At the same time, providers are rushing to integrate MAP with the other marketing technologies to make adoption of a unified suite of solutions even easier for companies. This is rapidly making technology-fueled, personalized selling the new standard of experience for consumers. That means that every company should work to deliver this kind of experience as soon as possible, or risk disappointing basic consumer expectations.

OUTBOUND

Build your own proprietary brand marketing network.

When a brand buys advertising from a website, TV network or magazine, they are essentially paying for exposure to the audience that the media company has gathered. In an ideal world, a brand would be able to collect its own audience of prospects and customers and not have to pay a third party for the privilege of sending messages to them. Getting your own database was difficult and laborious until the internet and email came along. The only way companies could collect physical addresses was through product registrations, catalogs, promotions, etc.

Brands can easily collect as big a database as they are able with digital registration, and can talk directly to this audience using email, with virtually no cost.

Owning a database of customers and prospects sets up the potential for what is essentially a proprietary brand marketing network. Amazon, of course, is the master of this, with its enormous database of 200 million customers, which is perhaps why you don't see many ads from them. It used to be that the segmentation of these in-house databases was a complex business requiring customized programming and development. Today, however, marketing automation software enables brands to segment down to the individual level with enormous flexibility. These systems also integrate with CRM platforms, which manage all the data that is thrown off by sales and customers. Together, these software platforms enable personalized drip marketing programs designed to cultivate prospects and customers based on their activity and interests.

DRIP MARKETING

Drip campaigns deliver much higher open rates and click throughs.

Drip marketing plans out the cadence of consumer touches based on the situation. A new lead might have a specific series of emails sent to them over a period of time. Customers might also activate a drip marketing sequence with specific actions that they take. The flexibility of MAP software allows brands to design these programs with great ease and supports their success with tracking and data, allowing for continuous optimization. Despite the new marketing bar that all this software has created, it doesn't mean drip marketing will work every time because the dynamics of consumer behavior vary greatly from industry to industry. It can, therefore, always benefit from a process of test, measure and refine.

Drip marketing is an old marketing idea with some new twists.

Drip marketing can be used to:

- Nurture leads
- Welcome new customers
- Get consumers to reconsider an abandoned shopping cart, (which happens an amazing 67% of the time according to Shopify)
- Deliver recommendations
- Get expiring customers to re-up
- Confirm orders and up-sell
- Get unsubscribes to stick around
- Keep people connected to your brand

9. PERMISSION EMAIL

THE GOLDEN GOOSE

Email is the only cost effective way to mass deliver personally relevant touches.

Central to the operations of these marketing automation platforms is email. Permission email, despite the spam plague that never seems to go away, has remained marketing's unsung hero through thick and thin. Even with new ways to communicate being introduced every day, consumers of all stripes just seem to prefer email. Now, with mobile taking over so much of our screen time, email even seems to be enjoying a renaissance with 91% of consumers checking their email at least once a day on their smartphone (ExactTarget), and according to a MarketingSherpa study, 72% of consumers say they prefer that companies use email, snail mail being a distant second with 48%.

Permission email has remained marketing's unsung hero through thick and thin.

Email has always been the perfect medium for brands: instantaneous, two-way, and dirt cheap. Today, with marketing automation software going mainstream, it is being recognized again for the gift to brands that it is. The opportunity of email is to have a direct channel to your customers and prospects at little to no cost. With every email, you can see how your recipient responds and track that information to help you make more effective emails in the future. With a big email database of the right people, who needs to pay for advertising? That has been the promise of email, but the problem has been that brands, just like people, don't value things that they don't pay for. Since email has always been so cheap, brands have thought nothing of spamming their own customers and prospects. If you only need a 1% response to give you a decent ROI, who cares if 99% of recipients don't respond. It's only when a large percentage of a database stops opening their emails that people sit up and take notice, usually too late. Too many emails, too little content value for the consumer, and an orientation towards the needs of the business (we need to sell more trucks this month!) versus the needs of the consumer, result in an injured and sometimes lifeless golden goose.

LIBERTY, NOT LICENSE

Just because email is cheap doesn't mean you can spam your customers.

Many brands successfully get people to give them their email address; it's actually a science in and of itself. It may be in exchange for content, which is how many marketing automation platforms are set up, or it may be as part of on-boarding a new customer. But instead of valuing this remarkable liberty to communicate with their consumers, many companies regard it as a license to bombard them with sales messages. They forget why these consumers signed up in the first place, which was usually in anticipation of receiving content which they would find valuable. Of course, the purpose of the exercise is to cultivate interest leading to sales, but the guiding principle should always be to put the interests of consumers first.

The more the individual recipient's needs and interests are prioritized, the better results you'll get.

Today's marketing software makes it easier than ever to target individual consumers with content that's exactly right for them. This results in 29% higher open rates and 41% higher click through rates according to Experian. Email is a very mature marketing channel with numerous vendors and platforms. This makes getting a sophisticated program up and running faster and easier than ever before. The challenge for brands is to first have the right strategies and planning in place to take advantage of the enormous potential of email and then to ensure that the effort is intelligently connected to their greater marketing system.

10. SUPPORTING TACTICS

SOCIAL MEDIA

Most consumers say that social media influences their purchase decisions.

Email may be the primary vehicle for nurturing leads, but it's not the only one. Social media, texts, direct mail, mobile apps and even good old-fashioned telephone calls, can all play their part in a comprehensive cultivation plan.

Social media is, of course, an excellent way to engage with prospects as well as consumers. We know that consumers value recommendations from their friends and others on social media more highly than anything else, so it would make sense to focus on it. Research from McKinsey & Co., for example, confirms that the impact of social media on decision-making is huge and growing. In some categories, such as travel or OTC drugs, they found 40%–50% of consumers looked to social media for guidance. They also found that first-time buyers are 50% more likely than repeat buyers to turn to social media, a finding that underscores how important a brand's social media can be. This is the case even though Facebook and others are turning social media into more of a Paid and Earned channel than an Owned channel.

Advertising is becoming the only way to reliably get a message to consumers in social networks, even those on your own page.

Unlike email, the dynamics of social media have become complicated by the big social media platforms. Facebook has narrowed, and almost entirely eliminated, the free access that brands have enjoyed to their own fan communities, a practice that other social networks seem to be following. That only leaves ads to reach Facebook audiences. While ads can be costly, they can still assist the nurturing process. If a known customer on your website explores a product but does not buy it, you can target an ad on Facebook to just that person. This is a form of re-targeting, an effective practice of advertising to people, by following them to other websites while their interest is still active. There are other things brands can do as well, such as simply placing sharing buttons on all their emails or using their MAP software to be alerted when known leads are actively researching your brand in social media. But short of paying for targeted ads, social media is proving to be less effective in the lead nurturing process, despite the hype, and lends itself more to brand awareness with shared content, such as with user-generated reviews.

MOBILE & MORE

Mobile has many marketing dimensions.

With the smartphone well and truly upon us, texting has gone from the domain of teenagers to a general communications channel. According to the Pew Research Center, 97% of Americans text at least once a day. Of course, a brand has to use it correctly. Text is not the medium for brand messaging or anything complex, but it can be excellent as one of a number of tactics to keep a brand top-of-mind, especially with time-sensitive communications. Texting is often best used as a trigger mechanism activating something else, such as a mobile app.

Mobile apps are another rich opportunity for most brands, but with thousands of underused or unused brand apps sitting in app stores, it is essential that brands think through the consumer rationale for an app before they invest in it. The purpose of a brand app is to provide consumers with functional value on an on-going basis. If an app only provides a one-time value it shouldn't be an app, it should be a web-based tool. Apps should be designed for repeated use. If they cannot deliver easier access to content, or some on-going functional value, then consumers will not waste time on them.

Will consumers really care about your app?

One app we developed for Allstate is an example of inserting a brand into consumers' lives. The app helps anyone easily inventory, store and keep updated a database of their personal belongings in the cloud, easily accessible in the event of a catastrophe. It guides consumers through the process of cataloging their home for insurance purposes by using their phone's camera. A challenging task that we've all set ourselves at one time or another now becomes easy and reliable, courtesy of the brand.

11. INTEGRATED CULTIVATION

BRANDS BEING HELPFUL

Consumers want marketing that is functional and useful.

Another project that we developed is instructive in describing how all these pieces can come together to cultivate customers and prospects. In looking at the garden and yard category for a large manufacturer of consumer seed and fertilizer products, we saw the opportunity to create a website destination focused on yards, not unlike how babycenter.com is focused on babies. The objective was to develop an indispensable aid to all yard owners. We did this by creating content that aligned with the yard-oriented search terms that the target audience were already looking for. This content would attract visitors through SEO and search. Visitors would discover not only original content but also numerous tools that would enable them to plan, upgrade and maintain their yards more easily. The content would attract visitors, the tools would keep them. This would lead to text and email recommendations on every subject relevant to them at just right moment, as well as timely offers.

A GREAT EXPERIENCE

Use your knowledge and expertise in your category to attract people and help them.

Consumer experiences usually start with a search, such as "How to edge a lawn." Video content that answers that question is more highly ranked because search engines give preference to video in search results. That's why content choices should be carefully researched to align with the most popular, but underserved and less expensive search terms, often called long-tail searches. A click on the search result take the viewer to the video on your website. Then, continuing our example, using their IP address and their computer clock, the system could recognize the time of day, the time of the year and the location of the viewer. That in turn would trigger content about yard conditions in their geographic area; it might be drier than normal, or spring planting time. Already, a first-time viewer would be getting a personally relevant experience by just showing up.

Brands that can find a way to help consumers reach their true goals, by simplifying or enhancing their lives, will earn a place in their lives.

The idea behind initiatives like this is simple: give your consumers reasons to stay connected with you. Use your knowledge and expertise in your category to attract them and help them. Learn about them from their behavior and use that knowledge to give them better solutions not just products. Consumers want beautiful tomatoes, not fertilizer; a stable retirement, not a Roth IRA.

CHAPTER 5

CLOSING THE DEAL

Convert prospects into customers

EXECUTIVE SUMMARY

This chapter is an overview of how modern marketing helps sales and marketing to work closer together to more effectively convert all their efforts into revenue. It is built on the foundation we have discussed in the preceding four chapters. If you have followed the process we have outlined, you are now ready to reap the benefits and convert your efforts into sales.

Conversion

- Remember the objective, directly or indirectly, is to get revenue.
- Digital tech enables an integrated selling system that merges marketing and sales.
- This is leading to e-commerce and DTC (direct to consumer) in almost every industry.

Connecting Marketing and Sales

- New technologies enable automated lead nurturing.
- Hand-offs to sales are smarter and more timely.
- Carefully choreographed engagement accelerates closes.
- It is essential to understand how trust is formed and how objections are overcome.

Digital Conversions

- Increasing digital conversion rates is faster and cheaper than growing traffic.
- Understand what drives conversion rates.
- Look for micro-conversions that will add up.

Lead Stages

- A lead takes a number of important steps before conversion.
- Information qualified lead (IQL) delivers personal information.
- Marketing qualified lead (MQL) identifies interest.
- Sales qualified lead (SQL) identifies someone ready to buy.
- Technology enables sales and marketing to automate much of this process.

Mobile

- Mobile is becoming a commerce medium.
- Brands need to get ready for a mobile commerce hockey stick.
- Keeping the pipeline full means playing the long game with many prospects.
- Response speed is an important factor in conversion.

Brand Website

- The brand website is the most powerful conversion tool in your arsenal.
- The elements have to be just right to encourage conversion.
- Continuous testing and experimentation is essential.

Cross-sell & Upsell

- It's easier to sell an existing customer than get a new one.
- CRM data informs cross-selling and upselling.

E-commerce

- It's easier than ever to enter the world of e-commerce.
- Tracking metrics will show you how to maximize performance.

Promotions

- There are lots of promo techniques to accelerate the closing process.
- As long as they don't become a drug, promos are valuable.

1. CONVERSION

CLOSING THE DEAL

> **Never forget that you are in the business of generating revenue.**

It is a common pitfall for marketers to get immersed in all the activity and forget that the purpose of our work is ultimately to generate revenue. At our agency, we forestall that to a large degree by having measurable KPIs (key performance indicators) against which we measure everything. This helps us remember that in the end, everything we do, directly or indirectly, has to produce measurable results for our clients—most often in the form of sales.

This chapter is about converting all your efforts into sales of one kind or another. As we outlined in Chapter 3, once a company has a thorough plan and a solid brand, the next step is to get awareness with some form of outreach. This initial contact with the consumer is then followed up with the methodical cultivation of each prospect, which prepares the ground for the moment when the prospect is ready to buy.

> **Everything we do, directly or indirectly, has to produce measurable results.**

Some marketers and agency people somehow divorce themselves from the idea that they are selling. It's like selling is beneath them, almost a bad word. Selling, however, is exactly what we do, and there is nothing wrong with it. It is simply the process of one person persuading another to their point of view, which, hopefully, promotes understanding and affinity in the process. As marketers, we should remember that we are in the business of selling and that our ultimate mission is to generate revenue. This is important to rember now that technology and data have closed the gap between marketing and sales and enable both to more effetiely accomplisy their mutual goal of generating revenue.

DIGITAL CONTEXT

The march to e-commerce, instead of slowing down, is just getting faster.

The relationship between marketing and sales has always been a testy one. Marketing typically feels like sales doesn't close enough of the leads they give them, and sales feels like the quality or quantity of the leads they get from marketing is inadequate. This all stems from the limitations that each discipline has traditionally been subject to, often due to the mediums and methods they had to work with. The evolution of the digital age, however, has removed many of those limitations, not only in how consumers interact with brands, but also in how the disciplines work, and work together.

The ability of technology-driven marketing to simulate consultative selling, combined with the power of automation, and behavioral data to improve timing and targeting, has resulted in a company being able to deploy an integrated system that can merge marketing and sales seamlessly. Naturally, the nature of what you are selling, and how it is purchased, determines what this system looks like. Some products need one-on-one sales interactions early in the sales cycle; some don't need any.

If sales is one-to-one and marketing is one-to-many, then modern marketing has become one-to-one-to-many.

Most electronics today are sold online without a salesperson ever being involved. Whereas a buyer used to go to Best Buy to explore the options with the guidance of a retail sales person, today they are more likely to consult online ratings and reviews, and then shop for the best deal without ever going near a store. While everyone used to use travel agents to buy airline tickets and hotel stays, now most of us pull up Expedia.com or Hotels.com and do it ourselves. And the march to e-commerce, instead of slowing down, is just getting faster, as digital experiences evolve to be able to simulate much more complex, consultative selling. Now even buying a car, a salesperson dependent ritual if ever there was one, is falling to the simplicity and convenience of digital selling. Some industries, like financial services, as we've mentioned before, have resisted this shift away from sales people. But as the burgeoning world of Financial Tech shows, there are few human interactions that technology cannot replace.

CHANGING CHANNELS

Almost any product that can be standardized is being sold direct through digital channels.

Not all automation, however, is considered an improvement by consumers. The rush to outsource call centers overseas delivered cost savings, but also unhappy consumers, which has led to a reverse trend bringing call centers back to the U.S. And who hasn't felt the frustrations of trying to get a computer voice on the telephone to understand your problem. The ongoing shift to automation, however, is being driven by multiple factors beyond cost savings, such as new consumer attitudes and behavior, especially among millennials. State Farm used to have a sales rep make every auto insurance sale. They believed, like most insurance companies, that the consumer's relationship with the agent was the key to keeping that business year in and year out. Then they automated the process, eliminated enormous swaths of cost, made everything simpler, faster, and more convenient for the consumer, and surprise, didn't lose the loyalty of their customers. In every industry, this transition from selling through agents, salespeople, or distributers, to digital selling, direct to consumer, has been challenging, but ultimately rewarding.

Protecting an existing revenue stream while growing a new DTC revenue stream is a delicate dance that companies have to master.

First, simple consumer products fell to e-commerce, as Amazon, with books and music, challenged the need for in-store guidance, and showed the world that the buying experience could be faster, easier, and more informed, to say nothing of cheaper. Now almost any product that can be standardized is being sold direct through digital channels. And even more complex sales that require planning and consultation are moving into the automated lane too. The work our agency has done for Pergo flooring, the originator of laminate flooring, allows a consumer to pick a new floor, get samples, figure out how much they need, order, arrange installation and even see what the floor will look like in their home using augmented reality technology, all without ever talking to a sales rep. Sure, consumers could go to the store, wait for a salesperson, and go through the same process, but why go to the trouble?

Consumers like e-commerce; it's also cheaper, faster, and produces valuable data for brands. That's why many companies are trying to get sales completed in digital channels, if possible. Since they are already, hopefully, driving new prospects to their website or social sites to present their value proposition, and using email and digital content to cultivate their interest, it only makes sense to close the deal in digital channels too. Of course, many products and services, especially in B2B, still require salespeople, but as we will see, even that has become more efficient as well.

2. CONNECTING SALES & MARKETING

ENDING THE WAR

Sales and marketing working together shortens sales cycles and reduces cost of sales.

CEOs would choose sales over marketing any day of the week, if they could. That's because they can easily see the cause and effect of a salesperson, whereas marketing traditionally has had less accountability. As a result, company cultures have separated sales and marketing into affiliated, but distinct, organizations that work fairly independently. At some point in the process, marketing hands off a lead to sales for qualification, cultivation and conversion, although that handoff is often imperfect, with little knowledge attached. Then salespeople follow their instinct to jump on the hottest leads, while often being less likely to invest the time and effort to develop cooler prospects. This sets up the probability that all but the best leads languish in sales limbo. Now, as we've described in previous chapters, marketing technologies allow companies to automate much of the follow-up process at a very sophisticated level. This enables salespeople to not only enter the process at exactly the right moment, armed with key customer insights, but also to tackle all the leads, not just the hot ones.

The opportunities for sales and marketing to work together to accelerate the entire sales cycle are becoming more accessible.

The automated cultivation of prospects enables a higher level of qualification before the handoff to sales. This delivers the lead at a point at which a salesperson may be actually required and desired by the prospect. Typically, the earlier stages of the selling process have been under the marketing umbrella and then, once sales takes over, they keep control from that point on. This too is changing, as it's now possible for marketing to assist sales throughout the entire sales process. For example, if you are renting apartments all over the country, like one of our clients, you need both marketing *and* sales to work together seamlessly throughout the process. Multi-family unit marketing relies heavily on digital channels, especially with predominantly millennial renters, but at some point, every would-be renter wants to visit prospective apartments to see for themselves what living there might be like. That's where salespeople become a pivotal link in the chain, with the ability to propel the sale or derail it.

CONSUMER EXPECTATIONS

No matter how hard companies try consumer expectations will continue to rise.

In the case of our multi-family rental client, most of the exploration and due diligence by prospects happens online. Millennials expect technology to deliver comprehensive answers to all their questions in an easy-to-use, engaging experience. They expect to be able to see how long their commute would be, what shops and restaurants are in the neighborhood and even what the view is from the bedroom window—all without the effort of visiting. This is the first challenge: to make sure that our client's rental properties get into the consideration set, and that our prospect's digital expectations are met and exceeded. But, no matter how compelling the digital marketing experience is, at some point the game switches to the real world with the tour of the property itself. That's why we work hard to ensure that the brand experience promised online translates into the real world. Inconsistency of brand experience denotes lack of authenticity and reliability. Not a good way to close a sale. Yet, even assuming an excellent impression during a tour, the actions we take with that prospect in the days and weeks that follow are equally critical to closing the deal.

Closing any sale is a mix of meeting needs, handling objections, building trust, staying in touch and timing.

Every product or service needs to have a carefully choreographed series of consumer engagements, or touches, from the first contact through final follow-up. It's a process informed by the knowledge of the prospect that you gather from the outset and throughout their journey. This is applied to each step that they take, building on previous steps, adding emotional and analytical impressions, which contribute to the overall brand perception that develops.

Coming out of any apartment tour, we can combine behavioral data about the prospect, gathered from their digital interactions before the visit, with what we learn about them during their visit. This can be used to shape a series of follow-ups focusing on the key considerations that we know are most important to them: the proximity of restaurants, the accessibility of internet services, or the walkability of the neighborhood. All contribute to not only keeping the brand top-of-mind during the time when a decision may be made, but also press the emotional buttons that are most likely to secure the conversion after the tour.

Our job as sellers is to reduce the complexity and increase the safety of the buying decision. To do that, we need to fully understand all the factors that a buyer considers in making a decision. We need to understand when and where emotions come into play as well as what analytical process might be at work. We then need to design our engagement strategy and messaging to make sure we meet the prospect's needs at every step and address objections along the way, all on a growing foundation of trust and confidence. If designed correctly, the sale itself becomes a natural extension of this process: another step in the journey that will continue on to loyalty and advocacy.

3. DIGITAL CONVERSIONS

LOSING SALES

Most company's online conversion rates are awful compared to the top 10% which are double-digits.

During our agency's initial discovery with new clients, one of the most common situations we uncover is that their conversion rates are low. They often have a good flow of traffic to their website and social sites, but their ability to convert that traffic into sales, or potential sales, is disappointing. This is usually because they do not have a systematic approach to qualifying, cultivating, and converting that traffic, which we have been discussing.

> **It only makes sense to try to first increase conversion rates, which are far more under your control, before spending additional money to develop more traffic.**

Traffic is difficult and expensive to create. While it is possible to create it organically, it often also requires pricey advertising. Conversion, by comparison, is inexpensive. The cost of researching the psychology of your prospects, planning an engagement strategy, automation and content software and even the team to manage it, is small compared to the cost of continually buying media to drive traffic that subsequently isn't converted.

LOW-HANGING FRUIT

> **Increasing your conversion rate will grow your company much faster that increasing your traffic.**

When someone invariably says, "What's the low-hanging fruit?" the answer is usually, "Improve your conversion rates." But conversion rates depend on many factors and can be misleading if not understood. Your conversion rates are a product of all the work you've diligently done, from your planning, to designing your brand, and implementing your marketing campaigns. But since so much of that work occurs in highly measurable digital channels, there are often many small things that you can do that will affect the overall conversion rate. These range from how you design your landing pages and forms, to fine-tuning content, response speed, and so on. The great news is this can be a very controllable process, where you can constantly test, measure, and improve.

This optimization process begins with careful study of the click paths that different personas take through your website and their key interactions along those click paths. Click paths show the choices that visitors to your website make. It's like a version of the sales funnel, with viewers choosing among options at each step. A study of these choices reveals whether viewers are doing what you want or expect them to do. Among these journeys are opportunities to increase the performance of many small interactions, or micro-conversions, by small amounts. Let's say a click path begins on a landing page. On the page are a number of choices. Some take the viewer further down the road toward a sale and some do not. While these choices rarely lead directly to a sale, they are important steps on the road. A small improvement at this point in the process will contribute to a higher conversion rate later. Together, many small improvements of, say, a tenth of a point each, quickly add up to serious increases in your overall conversion rate.

The result is that many small improvements to your content and user experience can have a big impact in aggregate.

While a focus on overall conversion rates for your Owned media, such as your website, is well and good, it is, however, too broad a brush to be useful in maximizing performance. Instead, you should focus on the micro-conversion rates for all the key steps that contribute to the overall sale. Conversion rate optimization works best when tied to these micro-conversions, such as viewing a landing page, watching a video, clicking a link or completing a form on a landing page; that's because they help your team focus on achievable, incremental improvement. Breaking conversion rates down further by referring channel, for example, will also help you better understand the dynamics of different audiences and acquisition channels, and will enable your team to better focus their efforts on your best opportunities.

This work requires a thoughtful approach because it is important to see the real significance of every action. For example, when consumers increase the frequency of visits because you make your site more engaging, that may not increase the frequency of buying. Instead, it could actually reduce your overall conversion rate, despite your success in strengthening your content. Another example might be the distortion that would be created if you included visitors, who are checking the status of their orders, or reviewing your "careers" page, in your overall conversion rate calculation. These scenarios underscore the importance of identifying and understanding what drives key conversion rates, and how they influence the final results you are seeking.

Closing the Deal

4. LEAD STAGES

INFORMATION QUALIFIED LEAD (IQL)

Despite its importance most companies spend little to nothing on the conversion process.

While ultimately a sale is what every company is always looking for, there are key steps in the process of turning a target consumer into a customer. Each is necessary and should be considered a victory. The first step, of course, is to successfully entice a target consumer to enter and explore your Owned media world, such as your website. This is the work we described in Chapter 3. The magic of your Owned media is that you control it. You don't have to pay others for access or ask permission to do anything. Your only master is your consumer.

Once a prospect enters your Owned world, the first conversion that you should seek is registration. The registration of people visiting your website, or responding to a marketing trigger, turns them into an *Information Qualified Lead* or IQL. Since everything you do in cultivation and conversion will be more effective if you can track the activity of a prospect who has been identified, this conversion should be a priority. Whether you plan to hand off to sales or close online, being able to communicate with the consumer as well as fully profile them, is enormously valuable.

Converting visitors into an IQL is usually done in exchange for some form of content. This may be a white paper, a newsletter, a video, a tip sheet, e-book or an application. The process is very dependent on compelling content, calls to action (CTAs) and the design of forms and landing pages. It's a process of enticement: presenting an offer that you judge to be sufficiently attractive to the viewer to motivate them to give you their contact information. This is given in exchange for a promise of value in return and is the beginning of a relationship with great expectations on both sides. As content marketing has proliferated, however, this exchange is, unfortunately, getting harder. As a result, the content and user experience bar for brands in search of IQLs is getting higher.

Consumers are developing a greater resistance to giving out personal information.

The prospect registrations that you get should be cherished. When consumers agree to connect with a brand and give their personal information in exchange for some promised content, it is a gift of great value to the brand. Consumers commit with the hope that what they will receive will be relevant, interesting, and useful. The brand is making an important branding promise to its consumers. The degree to which it succeeds in this promise will determine the consumer's ultimate perception of the brand.

Consumers hope that what you give them will help them and enhance their life. They are willing to open a channel with a brand in that hope, despite their reservations about making themselves known to yet another faceless corporate entity. No one wants the brand to succeed more than they do. On the other side, brands need that open channel with people who have a demonstrated interest in their products and hold the potential to become customers. The brand hopes that the consumer will engage with and respond to their communications and stay connected over time. It's a relationship based on hope on both sides, but that hope relies solely on the performance of the brand to succeed. From that moment on, it is up to the brand to make the relationship a success.

MARKETING QUALIFIED LEAD (MQL)

Smart scoring of leads delivers prospects at exactly the right moment.

IQLs are not qualified by anything other than the exchange of information that occurs. They are not necessarily hot, or even warm leads. They become part of a lead cultivation process, but are classified at a lower level because these leads have not yet exhibited any behaviors that would indicate they are potentially active buyers. However, this initial prospect identification begins the process and makes possible other conversions such as *Marketing Qualified Lead.*

The MQL assignment is based on scoring that allocates values to leads based on their activity and profile. A visitor to your website may come to win Super Bowl tickets. But if that's all they do, they may not be a good sales prospect. If, on the other hand, they also download product materials, your scoring will be different. Lead scoring is enabled by most Marketing Automation Platforms (MAP). An evaluation of consumer behavior data sets throughout their digital engagement with the brand, leads to activity profiles of prospects who are more likely to become customers. The system then scores all visitors on those activity criteria and can trigger different workflows, for example, a drip cultivation workflow, often consisting of a series of emails.

> An MQL is an identified lead who has met qualification criteria denoting it as a warm lead; not ready to buy perhaps, but worth an ongoing automated effort.

The key to the qualification process is the profile you build on each consumer. Bearing in mind the consumer's innate resistance to giving out information, many brands find the process of progressive profiling over time an effective way to build a rich, insightful profile. This is done by integrating landing page software, such as Unbounce, with CRM and MAP to collect additional information with each new interaction. For example, a lead scoring structure that we set up for a B2B client assigned points for the industry and title of the prospect. It gave values to the type of materials the person downloaded and the click path they took through the brand's website. It then gave higher values for reviewing certain content and information, like the contact page of the site. It also gave points for the number of emails opened and the number of clicks made within emails. The actual points awarded for each activity were based on our observations of the activities most likely to be associated with a person who ultimately became a customer. These can be extracted from large data sets of the behaviors of your customers. Some activities, like exploring the contact information of the brand, were assigned a point value that would quickly identify the visitor as a potential buyer and alert sales or trigger a workflow; many of the other criteria were not enough on their own to trigger an alert, but in aggregate would qualify a prospect.

SALES QUALIFIED LEAD (SQL)

> This is when you send the lead to your sales team.

While each company is different, a helpful concept for identification at this stage is BANT: Budget, Authority, Need and Timeframe. In most cases all four elements have to be positive in order for a lead to be considered ready to buy. Not all of this information is easily obtained, so it often takes multiple interactions, some even with marketing reps, to fully qualify the lead. These touches, however, become part of the six to eight touches that SalesForce and others say it takes to get the information you need to qualify an SQL. Clearly this is more relevant to more complex sales that require salespeople, particularly in B2B. But BANT is useful in developing SQL profile scoring based on behaviors that are likely to indicate a ready-to-buy prospect.

A sales qualified lead (SQL) is an MQL lead that has met the criteria that indicates it is potentially ready to buy.

From the point at which a lead is delivered to sales, the salesperson will drive the process. However, there are many circumstances, such as where the lead goes cool, in which it may again receive the attention of your automated cultivation system. As we've discussed before, if a lead runs through the process to sales and does not convert, it is usually smart to continue to stay in contact in the hope that it will turn warm again in the future. This is merely a matter of the lead being downgraded back to an MQL and continuing the automated outreach. Despite that, it is remarkable how many leads that have temporarily cooled are discarded. This is a reflection of a sales mentality, and it doesn't take into account that marketing will just have to go out and re-acquire that same lead at a later date at great cost.

5. MOBILE

A MOVABLE FEAST

Get ready now for the mobile commerce future.

In case you didn't notice, more people now access the web through mobile devices than through desktop devices. That changes how brands think about the consumer decision journey. At which interaction points are consumers on mobile devices? Do they want to complete transactions on their device? Are they just using mobile for research and then making the purchase later?

But this doesn't necessarily mean that everyone wants to complete every transaction in mobile, although according to Forrester, mobile commerce will rise to 33% of all U.S. e-commerce sales by 2020. The disconnect is that while, for example, almost a third of retailer traffic comes from mobile, it only delivers about 11% of sales. There are a number of reasons for this, including, slow mobile speeds, inadequate design of smartphone experiences, and poor integration of mobile into brand marketing systems.

> **The combination of tablet use, new sizes of devices, and better mobile user experiences supports consumer preference for their pocket computers.**

The move to mobile, however, marches on relentlessly, and the inevitable shift to mobile commerce is around the corner especially with 5G, the next geeration of wireless technology, coming. That's why brands should do what they can now to lay the groundwork for enabling mobile as a conversion channel. This includes investing in better mobile experiences, enabling easier access to product reviews, and making functionality in the conversion process easier, such as checking out and form completion. Research from the Columbia Business School tells us that 84% of shoppers use their phones to check prices and to look at reviews and additional information. Within a few short years most consumers will also expect to buy with them. They will expect simple, effortless ways to accomplish their tasks. Brands that do not prepare now to deliver on these expectations will soon find themselves at a disadvantage.

As Forrester reports, most of current mobile commerce activity takes place in apparel, consumer electronics and media. Much of it is also subject to multi-screen shopping. This is where shoppers research on mobile and complete the purchase on computers. While this will evolve with mobile overtime, it makes sense to make multi-screening easier today, with tactics like enabling saving or emailing a mobile shopping cart.

THE LONG GAME

> **At any time only a tiny percentage of prospects are ready to buy.**

Many prospects will buy something sooner or later; "later" sometimes being a very long while. That's why a big part of selling is always getting the prospect to accelerate the purchase and buy sooner. Great systems, persuasive value propositions, and consistent follow-up, will all contribute to getting more closes at any particular moment, but as we've noted earlier, many of the factors that ultimately influence a purchase may be out of the control of the brand, no matter what they do. The mission is therefore to build a system that consistently applies itself to every type of lead, from the hottest to the coolest, focusing energy on those ready to close, while not neglecting to reach out and engage all other leads.

> **Disciplined consistency over time creates a continuous pipeline of leads and is the secret to succeeding with these complex selling systems.**

Just ensuring that follow-up and "touches" do not stop after a couple of attempts can have a profound effect on conversions over time. If a prospect has consumed the value proposition, addressed concerns, answered questions and still does not buy, it does not mean that the game is over. On the contrary, the long game is just beginning. This is the process of feeding the interest that the lead has shown, maintaining awareness, growing trust and cementing brand preference in preparation for the moment when the consumer's need, desire and ability to act align. Brands that create marketing/sales systems that build an on-going pipeline designed to address not only short-term ready-to-buy consumers, but also the medium and long game of patiently cultivating prospects, will get that reliable revenue pipeline that they seek.

An important consideration in this is the type of content you should use for these long-term cultivation campaigns. This presents a problem in many categories because if a prospect is not in the market to buy now, then how do you keep them interested and your brand connected over time? One approach is looking at the general constituency of interest associated with the product. If your product is flooring, the general interest might be home improvement. If it's retirement investing, then anything to do with retirement is probably compelling. Finding the right hook to hang your content strategy on for the long game is a key that can unlock a rich pipeline over time.

SHOWROOMING & WEBROOMING

Most people Webroom and almost half Showroom.

With mobile use in retail environments growing, and mobile commerce growing, it is important for brands to understand how it will change the way people shop. For example, if you want to see a retailer look sad, talk about *Showrooming*. This is where people evaluate products in-store and then buy them later online, depriving the store of the purchase. *Webrooming*, on the hand, will make a retailer's smile return, because this is where the consumer researches online and then buys in-store.

A study from InfoScout on Black Friday shopping showed that 51% of shoppers admitted to webrooming versus 35% who said they were showrooming.

For brands that sell in brick-and-mortar locations, these dynamics are something to carefully watch as you craft the consumer journey around conversion points. Confident brands can, for example, facilitate Webrooming as a way to offer comprehensive research, an in-store experience and speedy gratification. Of course, all of this depends on the nature of your product or service.

SPEED

The faster you respond to a web lead the more likely you are to close it.

A classic Harvard study showed that of the thousands of companies they studied 24% took more than 24 hours to respond to a lead-initiated contact; 23% of the companies never responded at all.

According to leadresponsemanagement.org, the chance to qualify a lead drops to 10% after the first hour, and after 10 hours leads are invariably completely cold.

While many brands might use a call center for this follow-up, some use automated email or even text, which can also be an effective tool. A study by Velocify, for example, showed that sending a text immediately after an initial contact increased subsequent conversion rates by 112.6%.

6. BRAND WEBSITE

THE ENGINE OF GROWTH

Your website is your most valuable marketing asset. Nothing comes close.

Owned media is the engine of your modern marketing system, and the crown jewel of your owned media is your website. No other asset offers more potential and versatility in your mission to cultivate and convert prospects than your website.

Visits to your site may be from paid search, content marketing in social channels, email, or advertising. Once those visitors arrive, your website should be designed to segment them, and then present them with the most tailored value proposition possible. There are many ways to do this, which we discussed in the last chapter, but all of this is only in preparation for converting the visitor either to a customer, or to a key stage on the way to becoming a customer.

All your initial efforts should be designed to get target consumers to go to your website.

Your brand website is the best place to take prospects through the process of learning about your product or service, discovering why it is the right choice, and enabling an easy process of becoming a customer. While some of these things can be done in other channels, such as on your social websites or on an app, your brand or company website is still the place where you can create the most persuasive and compelling experience. Of course, there are probably other things that you might want your website to do. These include serving the needs of your existing customers, and providing information for recruiting, investors or press. But these other functions of your website should not cause you to minimize the ability your site has to act as your storefront and best salesperson. Modern user experience design (called **UX**), when combined with the strategy work outlined in Chapter 1, will show you how to create a website that can serve multiple masters while not losing sight of its primary purpose.

THE SUCCESS FORMULA

Keep experimenting and testing because what works is constantly changing.

Conversions on your website will be driven by many factors that contribute to a great experience for the prospect. Here are a few to consider:

1. **Calls-To-Action**—CTAs in critical areas throughout the site.

Asking for the order frequently, yet respectfully, is basic sales psychology.

It is impossible to predict the moment when a tire-kicker becomes a buyer, so make sure there are CTAs (calls to action) in all critical spots on your website as your value proposition unfolds. Remember that presenting the pitch will probably happen in two to five steps. At each of these stages the CTA may be presented differently based on what you have observed about the visitor's behavior, but the simple idea is to be appropriate for the context and make it easy for the buyer to buy.

2. **Content**—answering consumer questions and attracting search.

For content to influence conversion it should be carefully tuned to the stage at which the prospect is at.

Content drives prospects through the value proposition, which makes it a key consideration in maximizing conversion. As we have discussed in previous chapters, content always needs to be compelling, which means it should be as tightly tied to the specific interests of that prospect at that moment as possible. It should also be designed to support the process rather than hinder it. That's why a branding video at the shopping cart stage could be a negative, since it would slow the process and deflect the buyer's focus from the task at hand.

3. **Landing Pages**—optimized for target consumers

Conventional wisdom holds that 10% of landing pages deliver 80% of conversions.

Landing pages are where visitors to your site often arrive. Brands with sophisticated marketing operations usually engineer the vast majority of website visitors to arrive at landing pages versus the home page. That's because landing pages are designed to speak to the mindset of the particular prospect, and, as such, are more relevant, persuasive and compelling. Landing pages are the best way to address specific audiences according to their own needs. As Sheena Iyengar, a psycho-economist at Columbia Business School discovered, the alternative, a plethora of choices on the home page, reduces the propensity to buy by as much as a factor of six. Some actually argue that landing pages that live outside of your website further increase the singular focus of the page and reduce the negative effects of "online ADD."

Having fewer, more effective landing pages argues for a comprehensive testing process to quickly discover the winners and weed out the poor performers. Part of this process should be to constantly test, because even successful landing pages go stale over time as other factors change and influence their effectiveness. That's why brands need a comprehensive, ongoing landing page development and testing plan and process.

4. **Testimonials** — leveraging the credibility of other consumers

There is nothing quite as believable as the voice of the consumer.

Consumers understand clearly that brands are trying to sell them something, and even the least sophisticated buyers take Brand Promises with a grain of salt. That's why, in this age of "trust but verify," where consumers expect to confirm the truth from third parties, the onus is on brands to provide credible references. There are many ways to do this, but none quite as emotionally powerful and believable as the honest words of your customers. These are not actors pretending to be customers reading carefully prepared scripts, because most of us, on some level, can spot fake sincerity and will give it the credibility it deserves. Testimonials are not a small consideration.

Consumers cry out for believable third-party validation for their decisions. Without it, they are not only uncomfortable in making purchases, but also really frustrated at their inability to get the answers they want. They are also grateful to any organization that solves that problem for them.

The three ways to tackle testimonials:

- **Video**—Interview your customers on video. People believe real people who are speaking in their own words. Never try to get them to read a script. They won't be able to do it well and the audience will see through it. You can, however, edit interviews to your heart's content, which allows you to shape the message. Also, as we know, people prefer videos, just remember to keep them short, easy to consume, and don't strain credibility by incorporating any sales messages.

- **Audio**—If you can't get your customers on camera because of scheduling, distance, or cost, record an interview with them over the telephone. Remember it is the voice of the consumer that has the power. You don't need to see someone's face to know that their words are real and credible; you can hear it. This is a far less expensive proposition than video, yet equally effective. Match it up with a photo of the speaker and make sure, once again, that it is not too long.

- **Text**—A distant third is text quotes from customers. These don't have the visceral power of audio or video and without that emotional truth feel much less believable.

5. **Ratings & Reviews**—the most common third-party validation

Study after study shows that over 90% of consumers use ratings and reviews to help make their decisions.

This is how self-assured companies demonstrate their confidence and transparency today. That's why ratings and reviews should be prominently displayed and show the good, the bad and the ugly. Don't be afraid of bad reviews, in fact they are an opportunity. Just like a customer service problem can show in social media that you listen, care and respond to issues, so too can ratings and reviews show your transparency and customer orientation. Be sure to show your solution for anything negative right there with the review. That is a powerful demonstration of your commitment, concern, and responsiveness.

Be careful, however, that your reviews don't look too rosy, because studies show that consumers might think something is fishy. They know that reviews can be manipulated, and so they look for common sense signs that reviews are honest. Of course, that doesn't guarantee they will be, but be alert to how yours appear. There are a number of ratings and reviews platforms such as Bazaarevoice, which can be easily integrated into your owned media.

6. **Third-Party Press**—more external validation

Capture, share and display social posts that reinforce your brand.

Like reviews or testimonials, articles or press about your brand have the air of objectivity. If your brand is favorably mentioned in the press, by all means use it on your site, share it with your prospects and generally enjoy the credibility it confers. This can be engineered, of course, with PR and good relationships with the press, which should be an ongoing effort if budget allows. Related to PR is social media commentary. This too confers an objective third-party credibility. When customers, reviewers, and others talk favorably about your company or brands, their posts can provide another source of valuable objective validation. Sprinkle them throughout the sales experience and especially as the conversion stage approaches. Make clear where they come from and give them the raw look of a real post for added credibility.

7. **Quantifiable Claims**—make it real

Vague promises, untestable claims and exaggeration will not impress skeptical consumers, and will not assist your mission.

Research confirms that the use of numbers, almost any numbers, bestows credibility on the subject matter at hand. People just seem to believe numbers, because they appear to represent objective truth. Therefore, wherever possible use numbers, and always make their sources clear. This is part of an increasing consumer orientation in favor of claims that appear quantifiable and measurable versus unaccountable. Also, while we are talking about numbers, there is evidence that different numbers in various contexts can have unusual effects, such as the power of the number nine. Hence the preponderance of price points one cent or one dollar less than the round number. If your brand is very e-commerce-oriented, this is an area worth digging in to as well.

8. **Consistency of Brand** — communicates reliability

Consumers are alert to signals of a lack of authenticity.

This includes inconsistency of language, offers, branding, and even design. Before the sale everything a brand does is a clue for the prospect as to how the brand might conduct itself later. Clearly positives will help the conversion, while negatives will hurt. Consistency is a subtle signal that consumers will pick up on, even if only on a subconscious level. All the little signals that a consumer detects eventually add up to a larger perception, and it's the brand's job to ensure that every detail is thought through and deliberate. This is especially important in the final stages of closing a sale where the prospect's sensitivity to inconsistent branding and negative signals will grow.

9. **User Experience** — makes it easy

Testing different permutations against subsets of an audience is the only way to ensure that something is working as well as it can.

An effortless, intuitive experience is another critical signal that the prospect uses to determine what it's going to be like to be a customer. User experience, or UX, is a mix of science and art that determines the most effective ways to present content. It is the study of the minutiae of how and why consumers make choices in digital experiences and beyond. It influences not only the way digital experiences are designed, but also how products are designed. In digital channels UX predicts what the user will do, and want to do, at any particular moment, and what the most efficient and satisfying experience might be.

There is much attention paid to the effect of the subtleties of UX in website design, particularly as it pertains to conversion experiences. The placement of a button, or its color, might produce different consumer responses, which can and should be measured and evaluated. This process of testing different UX-led designs is one of the critical methods that a brand should use to maximize the effectiveness of any particular step in a conversion path.

It's also an essential part of the process of finding many small improvements in performance that in the end add up to significant improvements in conversion. All consumers want digital experiences, whether on a smartphone or a computer, that are fast, easy, intuitive and delightful. Designers look to UX professionals, in conjunction with strategists, to guide them to the perfect mix of elements and design to accomplish this.

7. CROSS-SELL & UPSELL

USING DATA

> Your ability to track and use data will determine your marketing success.

CRM platforms enable brands to track and store behavioral data about customers. Customers produce a great deal of data that can give you insights not only into the behavior and potential actions of a particular customer, but also, when viewed as datasets, can predict behaviors of different categories of customer.

> Data can tell you the right thing to pitch next, and when to pitch it.

CRM data, combined with marketing automation data, can tell a brand what the activity of a prospect or customer is likely to be within the brand's eco-system. When married to recommendations based on analysis of preferences for large numbers of customers, this can result in very effective lifecycle management. CRM platforms are increasingly integrated with MAP, marketing automation platforms, which is only logical and a big step forward in unifying the entire marketing technology suite.

CROSS-SELLING

> If you are not cross-selling you are missing a big opportunity for added revenue.

Upselling happens at the point of sale versus cross-selling, which should be part of an on-going customer strategy. According to Forrester, upsells and cross-sells can deliver as much as 30% of e-commerce revenues. As Wells Fargo has demonstrated, cross-selling works, although, as we know, it is also a cautionary tale. While hundreds of thousands of customers were persuaded to buy other products, the culture of sales at any cost was inevitably revealed. The resulting loss of trust for their brand is far greater than any revenue they received and demonstrates that in everything, brands must put their customers first or suffer the wrath of the community.

Cross-selling should be very strategic and driven by behavioral data if it is to be successful.

Behavioral data starts by delivering an understanding of which segments and personas are worth pursuing and which are not. These segments could be groups that tend to overuse customer service, limit their spending, or only take advantage of steep incentives or promotions. This is very important to know because all cross-selling is not necessarily good. As a study by Georgia State University in the *Harvard Business Review* revealed, "Cross-selling is profitable in the aggregate. But one in five cross-buying customers is unprofitable—and together this group accounts for 70% of a company's customer loss." The moral of this story is, therefore, be sure that the customers you target with your cross-selling efforts will be profitable customers.

Assuming you have identified your potentially profitable segments, then comes the determination of what to sell next to each person. If a bank customer only has a credit card, a retirement account may not be the next financial product she will want to consider, but an auto loan might be. Analysis of large datasets of customer behavior patterns will reveal potential answers. This should be followed up with targeted research to confirm your insights. The result should be a data-driven profile for your best potential segments. You should then apply this to your CRM database to identify those prospects that match. Once in place, you wait for your marketing automation platform to alert you to preset trigger behaviors from matching candidates that indicate a prospect who qualifies. That's when you fire off your offer: the right offer, to the right person, at the right moment.

UPSELLING

Proven techniques lead to considerable increases in order size.

Upselling is different to cross-selling. It's what it sounds like: persuading a customer to buy a more expensive item or make their purchase bigger with additional products. Unlike cross-selling, it happens within the window of a purchase that is already being made, or has recently been made. There are lots of upselling techniques, but some that you may have seen most often are social proof recommendations such as "Customers also bought…," or *Bundling*, where you offer packages at special rates, which ups the order size. Attracting interest with a low price and presenting buyers with more expensive options at the checkout is another common technique used by upsellers. JetBlue, for example, encourages passengers when they are completing their purchase to stretch their legs with their "Even More Space" option. Since 2008, when it was introduced, they have more than quadrupled revenue to over $200 million from this source alone.

Upselling not only produces larger orders and more revenue, but also better satisfaction with customers who are happy that you are making relevant and useful recommendations.

Tactics like showing how much a customer can save, or offering free delivery for an additional purchase, can boost results too. Eyewear brand ToyShades increased conversion 113% and the size of orders by 16% by adding a "popular" category on product pages and upsell suggestions at checkout. Upselling can be relatively simple, such as associating products together, or complex, such as offering upsells that are driven by individual profiles. Start simple and grow more complex as you accumulate data and your team gets experience.

8. E-COMMERCE

BEING DIRECT

E-commerce continues to grow and is poised for another explosion in growth.

Most companies that can easily sell their products or services online are probably already doing so. Not long ago, setting up e-commerce was expensive and complicated, but now thanks to software platforms like Shopify, brands can be up and running quickly and inexpensively. However, while these providers have made e-commerce very accessible, especially for smaller companies, there are still many nuances that separate top operators from the rest. Many products and services still rely on legacy distribution systems of one sort or another, and many others don't lend themselves to the relative simplicity of e-commerce. But e-commerce continues to grow and is poised for another explosion in growth as artificial intelligence and other technologies are injected into the process.

The key to successful e-commerce is ease of use, speed, and how delightful you can make the experience.

Clearly, consumers continue to get more comfortable with the convenience of e-commerce every year, and this trend is not going to stop anytime soon. Before long we can expect that even the most complex purchases, *considered purchases* that have before always required the guidance of a salesperson, will migrate online. The implications for companies stuck in outdated distribution systems, "middle-men" sellers and distributors, point to another titanic shift in the marketplace. With the technologies that will drive this next wave of change just arriving, the good news is that there are already a wealth of options, information and guidance available that can make upgrading or entering the current e-commerce world relatively fast and painless.

FORMS & ABANDONMENT

Small investments in form design can lead to large increases in conversion rates.

One would think that by the time people opt to check out the sale has been made and the rest is just mechanics. Why then do the majority of people who fill out conversion forms abandon them? This is actually true of most kinds of forms, and points to a variety of issues and challenges that revolve around design, privacy, price and security. The good news is that you can measure each step in the form-completion process fairly easily so that you can know where abandonment happens and start to address issues and opportunities with those insights.

Remember that someone filling out a shopping cart form or another type of conversion form may not be completely sold yet.

That's why it's important that you make sure you include some of the third-party validation elements we reviewed earlier. These are designed to give the buyer confidence in their decision at this critical juncture in the process. Also, be sure to directly address the issues of privacy, price and security. Privacy is often a concern related to the potential, unwanted attentions of salespeople, or unsolicited sales messages, that might come from sharing personal information. Consumers may need to be reassured that outreach to them will not be intrusive or that they will have some control. Reassuring them with privacy policies and clear statements of what they can expect will allay possible fears. Likewise, in our world of hackers, people need to be reassured very clearly and credibly about the security of their personal information. In some circles, this is considered the top consumer issue; in the light of the numerous data breaches experienced by major retailers, every company should address this challenge as best they can.

Finally, do not leave pricing until the last moment in the process because the surprise it can represent may derail the sale. As we mentioned before, introduce pricing early, especially shipping costs, and if necessary combine it with price assurances, such as best price guarantees. This can allay the fears of the jittery buyer, who is intent on finding the absolute best deal, and may hesitate to complete the transaction until they have confidence that they have made the best choice. As the final stages of a sale approach, the last thing that a brand wants is for buyers to feel the need to stop and go back to researching in order to be absolutely sure they are getting the best deal. They may not come back.

FORM DESIGN

Less is more when it comes to form design.

Form design is, in itself, a science and an art. Just look at any form produced by the IRS and you can see how the design of a form can cause a consumer to run for the hills. First, make sure that you are only asking for information that you absolutely need, and the less you ask for, the better. All too often brands ask for all the information they could possibly want, seemingly oblivious to the fact that consumers don't have to give it to them. How many times have we all confronted overly long forms where virtually every line is marked required? Consumers understand that a company needs, for example, an email address to send them the whitepaper they would like to read. But they may ask themselves, "Why do they also need a telephone number, mailing address, title, company, and shoe size?" Rather than forking over your personal information, you decide the white paper isn't worth the potential trouble and abandon the form. The result, is the brand has nothing to show for the interaction—which it paid to get.

It doesn't take a rocket scientist to figure out that by giving a brand lots of personal information, you are setting yourself up for a sales attack.

Another way to think about gathering information is incrementally. Say you only get the email address and first name of your prospect during your first interaction. Now you are able to communicate with the prospect, and in subsequent communications, you can ask for additional pieces of information. Each small request may in itself seem innocuous, and produce very simple forms, but over time you can build a deep, rich profile, without alarming the prospect.

Form design is also about the experience itself. How easy is it to complete? How much does it self-complete? For example, if you enter your ZIP Code, it can automatically populate the city, state and shipping cost. The emotional experience of the form tells the prospect what it may be like to be a customer. If the form is overwhelming, complex, one-sided and confusing, then perhaps this might not be a company to work with. The bottom line is to use content and design to allay fears, make the experience of the form fast and simple, and remove trust or convenience barriers as much as possible.

9. PROMOTIONS

GOOSING SALES

The majority of consumers hunt for promotions on the web.

Much of the work of modern marketing is about creating and identifying leads. But often, companies just can't wait for the cultivation process to unfold naturally. That's when they step in with techniques designed to stimulate both lead generation and sales. All of this falls under the broad umbrella of promotions. Promotions are designed to give consumers an incentive to act sooner rather than later—or often within a designated time period. This, of course, is one of the fundamental missions of sales: to get prospects to accelerate a purchase and buy on the brand's schedule rather than theirs. It's fair to say that you're going to buy a car at some point in the future, but the salesperson wants you to buy that car within the next three months.

Too frequently promotions can quickly devalue a brand and shift the value proposition from value to price.

Promotions are how brands get consumers to change their timetable by presenting them with an incentive to act now. Promotions include offers around price, content, service and other value add-ons. There are many other promotional ideas, of course, and this is an area that lends itself to creativity. The idea is always to find new ways to stand out for short periods of time and spike sales. Promotions, however, can be a trap. Used occasionally on top of branding and cultivation strategies, promotions are an effective tool to smooth out business cycles. When used too frequently, promotions can quickly devalue a brand and shift the value proposition from value to price; that's usually a dangerous trap.

Promotional tactics—an incomplete list:

- **Discounts**—discounts can be time specific, while supplies last, or just sales priced.
- **Vouchers and coupons**—time-limited, online, in store, in publications, email.
- **Finance deals**—discounted financing or no payments until…
- **Buy-One-Get-One-Free (BOGOF)**—two for one.
- **CRM offers**—feeding loyalty with bonus points or coupons.
- **Free shipping or faster shipping**—can be tied to a transaction minimum amount to protect margins. Both are an incentive to act now.
- **Free returns**—can be tied to free shipping or stand alone. You can incorporate the cost into the price.
- **Flash sales**—all about a very short limited time. According to Monetate 50% of purchases happen within the first hour of flash sales.
- **Branded gifts**—a free pen flashlight with every purchase over $100. Limited quantities.
- **Price match**—a powerful promise that takes the price risk out of the equation.
- **Holiday promotions**—a great excuse for a promotion. Less potential for damaging brand price integrity.
- **Competitions and sweepstakes**—in any channel, in addition to packaging in-store.
- **Cause-related**—raise money for charities and causes with or without purchase.
- **Free samples**—sampling at events or high traffic locations.
- **Promotional tie-ins**—fast-food restaurants give away movie toys with kid meals.

CHAPTER 6

WINNING THE MARATHON

Keep customers and turn them into advocates

EXECUTIVE SUMMARY

It's so difficult and expensive to acquire customers that the last thing you want is to lose them. Instead, the idea is to keep and grow your relationships and their value over time. This is also your opportunity to convert customers into fans who will spread the good word about your brand to new prospects.

Retention Pays

- Retention dramatically affects profitability.
- Loyalty is not dead, it's just different.
- Customers expect flawless, effortless, pleasing experiences.
- Brands must turn customers into advocates who will promote them to their networks and defend them when issues arise.

Customer Lifetime Value

- Understand what a lead is worth, what a customer is worth, and how much to invest in acquisition and development.
- Calculate CLV for each persona.
- Focus on segments which are profitable.
- Invest in the systems, people and processes required to retain today's consumers.

Net Promoter Score

- NPS, from Bain & Co, has become the gold standard of customer happiness.

- By the time you find out if a customer is unhappy the damage is done.
- NPS leaders grow, on average, at twice the rate of competitors.
- NPS, or something like it, needs to be a core component of any customer retention and development plan.

Lifecycle Planning

- Each target segment, and even each individual, needs to have a lifecycle plan.
- Understand the purchase cycle for each persona.
- Map lifestyle stages for each persona and category.
- Like everything else Lifecycle Planning is enabled by data and your organization's ability to interpret it.
- The plan tells you what to sell next at every step.

Customer Retention

- It costs up to seven times, or more, to acquire versus retain a customer.
- Identify those customer segments that have the greatest lifetime profit potential.
- Follow three core strategies: Know your customer, Reward their loyalty, Make their lives better.
- Follow the new rules of brand behavior.

Customer Service

- Every customer interaction becomes an extension of your culture and a metaphor for your brand.
- Brands require a new level of sensitivity and responsiveness to consumer needs and feelings.
- Connecting with a brand should be easy and delightful.
- Be careful cutting CS costs. This is not the area to be less than great.

Data Integration

- Consumers expect brands to know what's going on.
- Connect your data dots so the left hand knows what the right hand has done.

- Only with comprehensive systems integration can a company and its brands behave the way consumers want and expect.

Advocacy

- The social media power of individuals to determine the fate of a brand is enormous.
- Actively encourage and enable your customers to become advocates.
- Make advocacy easy.

Loyalty

- The goal is the retention and growth of profitable customers.
- Loyalty data and insights are more valuable than simple retention.
- Loyalty programs are increasingly using experiences to differentiate the brand.
- A loyalty program needs to develop its own branding and strategy.

---

1. RETENTION PAYS

WHY CUSTOMERS STAY

In order to super-serve your customers you need to truly understand them.

With the shift of power from companies to consumers, brands have few options but to super-serve their customers. This means doing the work to truly understand them and using those insights to deliver the products, services and brand experiences that will exceed their expectations. The challenge for many smaller firms is that consumer expectations of what good brand experiences are have continued to rise. This has been driven by large brands investing heavily in new levels of brand experience, often digital, designed to give them an edge by smoothing out customer interactions, anticipating every need, and being delightful in the process. This has caused many consumers to expect equally flawless, effortless experiences from all their vendors, not just the big ones.

> The challenge for many smaller firms is that consumer expectations of what good brand experiences should be have skyrocketed.

In the preceding chapters, we outlined how to harness processes and technology to deliver on these new expectations. We explained how these digitally savvy, socially adept buyers reward companies that deliver what they need and want, and how they punish those that fail, or break the new rules of brand engagement. The good news is that doing the right things not only gets the sale, but will also earn social media power, which in turn translates to loyalty, advocacy, and by extension, greater lifetime value from each customer.

THE NEW LOYALTY

> Loyalty is earned by brands that do the work daily to deserve it.

There are some who would argue that brand loyalty is dead and that most consumers don't want relationships with brands, whatever that means. But many brands, from Uber to Apple are actually redefining what brand loyalty in the 21st century means. It certainly isn't the blind loyalty of old, where you buy the same car your grandfather did, just because. Instead, loyalty today is earned daily by brands that are willing to do the hard work to deserve it. It's a simple formula, consumers want to do business with companies that have the quality and prices they want, that are predictable, reliable, easy to work with, and that share their values. Consumers are enabled by the internet, which has made the process of continuous evaluation increasingly easy, and by the empowerment of technology, which has melted away inertia. But, in today's social media-fueled world, even happy, loyal customers are not enough. Brands must turn them into advocates and ambassadors who will spread the word on their networks, share their enthusiasm, and defend them when issues arise.

> Many brands from Uber to Apple are redefining what brand loyalty in the 21st century means.

Growing lifetime value, loyalty and advocacy are the focus of this chapter. As with previous subjects covered in this book, we are looking at the new consumer dynamics that have shifted basic marketing models and which are unlikely to change until the next massive shift; hopefully not before you've finished this book. Of course, fads will come and go, and tech breakthroughs will capture our attention for a while, but the underlying dynamics of this new commercial age, which are so different from before, are unlikely to change again in the near future.

2. CUSTOMER LIFETIME VALUE

HOW TO CALCULATE IT

All your customers are not worth the same.

Acquiring a customer is an expensive and competitive business. Of course, there is nothing else to talk about if a brand can't attract prospects and convert them into customers. But assuming that process is working, what then? What is that customer worth? How can you keep them, grow their spending, as well as tap their referral power? Every company must be asking these questions and strategizing how to maximize the lifetime value of each customer.

The Customer Lifetime Value calculation enables marketing organizations to budget their acquisition efforts correctly.

This starts with determining your current customer lifetime value (CLV). If you've been in business for a while, you should have the data to do the calculations. CLV is, in effect, a prediction of the profit you expect to generate from customers in the future, over an entire customer lifecycle, based on historical data. While the idea has been around as long as companies have had customers, it was really enabled by the advent of ERP and CRM software, which allows companies to easily keep track of customer data.

CLV takes into account the profit a customer is likely to generate, less the associated costs of acquisition and service. This value enables marketing organizations to budget their acquisition efforts correctly by understanding what a lead is worth, what a customer is worth and how much to invest in acquisition. It's informed by lead-to-conversion rates, the cost associated with generating a lead and the value of a sale.

GO WHERE THE MONEY IS

Determining CLV lets you target your efforts to your best prospects.

The process of exploring the financial value of your customers lets you identify segments that are more profitable or active than others, segments where churn might be happening and why, and what the potential for sales in the future might be. A solid CLV will bring discipline and business-led parameters to your customer acquisition and retention efforts, as well as enable more reliable business planning.

It quickly becomes clear that it is cheaper to sell more to existing customers than it is to acquire new ones.

If you have clearly distinct segments of customers, or types of purchase, each should have the CLV calculated separately. Each calculation should be based on the average length of time in years that a customer remains active, and the average annual profit from sales to that customer type, less the average cost to acquire both the first sale and then each subsequent sale. You will need to know the average number of sales in a lifetime too. These measures will inform not only the CLV number, but let you know how much you can spend to initially acquire a customer, and then how much you should invest to get subsequent sales. In most instances, it will quickly become clear that it is cheaper to sell more to existing customers than it is to acquire new ones. We've all heard that this old saw, but it's much more meaningful when you see it confirmed with your own numbers.

Invariably what you end up with argues for investment in the systems, people and processes that will give you the data and insights you need to retain customers and grow the amount of business you do with them.

3. NET PROMOTER SCORE

THE MAGIC QUESTION

Develop a customer early warning system.

Before we break down retention and loyalty into their component parts, a good subject to discuss is NPS or Net Promoter Score, a measure devised by Bain & Co. This measurement has become the gold standard of customer happiness, retention and lifetime value potential, and as such, something like it should be a part of your process.

All companies want happy customers, operating on the assumption that in most instances this leads to stronger, longer relationships and more business. The problem has been that usually by the time you find out if a customer is not happy, or even worse, unhappy, the damage may already be done. This was the situation that Fred Reichheld, author of the seminal book *The Loyalty Effect,* and his employer, Bain & Co., set out to solve by testing different ways to reliably predict customer behavior. What they landed on was a single, simple question that, in most situations, would deliver a reliable prediction of future customer behavior. The question was: *What is the likelihood that you would recommend Company X to a friend or colleague?*

Net Promoter Score leaders grow, on average, at twice the rate of competitors.

It's a deceptively simple question, but what it is essentially asking is, would you put your reputation on the line based on the experience you have had with this company? As it stood up to test after test in numerous industries, what soon became apparent to the Bain researchers was the power of this question to predict behavior. Since then, repeated Bain studies have found that Net Promoter Score leaders grow, on average, at twice the rate of competitors.

REFERRAL POWER

Referrals are the currency of business.

As we all know, referrals in every business are usually one of the greatest sources of sales, but now, in our social media–enabled world, they have become the currency of business. People realize the power of their recommendations. They understand that their opinion has value and they have become comfortable expressing themselves. The Net Promoter Score manages to capture the emotional essence of these recommendations and opinions into a single answer, giving brands critical insight into the trust and confidence that they have to earn in order to win, and keep, their consumers.

People realize the power of their recommendations.

NPS is valuable for virtually any company. It's simplicity and ease of execution, combined with its easily understood insights, have earned it a huge following. This has become very timely just as social media has made it essential to know how you are doing with every single customer, all the time. From Apple stores and American Express, to Logitech and Charles Schwab, companies use NPS as an early warning system. When inevitable mistakes happen, or execution is under par, NPS can spot the trouble and indicate how to repair it before it does too much damage or hits social media. Without NPS, or something similar, a company is flying blind at a time when customers are making more demands, have higher expectations, and have the ability to share their feelings at their fingertips. That's why NPS, or something like it, needs to be a core component of any customer retention and development plan.

HOW IT WORKS

Identify and turn around passives and detractors.

NPS scores fall into three general categories: promoters, passives, and detractors. Each is what it sounds like, and your organization should respond accordingly. The process is simple. Customers score their answers on a score of "0–10", "0" being not at all likely to recommend and "10" being extremely likely. Promoters gives you a score of "9" or "10", passives are either "7" or "8", and "6" and below are detractors. The percentage of promoters less the percentage of detractors is your Net Promoter Score.

The secret is the execution and that means getting buy-in from your troops.

The good news is that there is a great deal of knowledge about NPS available, including benchmarks for many industries, so getting a program off the ground quickly is very possible. As with most things, however, the secret is the execution, and that means getting buy-in from your troops. Even with insightful data such as NPS, in hand, it takes a committed organization to turn detractors around, and to turn passives into promoters. Making NPS a part of your regular interactions with your customers also communicates your ongoing commitment to excellence, which in itself is an important message.

4. LIFECYCLE PLANNING

THE PURCHASE CYCLE

Start with the basic dynamics of your category.

Armed with the ability to measure customer happiness reliably and often, a brand should turn its attention to keeping more customers and growing their value. This starts with understanding the customer purchase cycle for your industry, product category or target audience. Automobiles used to have a two- to three-year purchase cycle, but now according to AutoMD, many people plan to drive their cars past the 100,000-mile mark. Clearly, how a product is consumed determines its sales cycle. In days past, the milkman would deliver fresh milk every day and chalk up another sale. On the other hand, buy a top-shelf refrigerator and you get a guarantee for 20 years.

Purchasing dynamics clearly affect how a customer should be marketed to and what their lifetime potential might be.

If the challenge is to continue to get someone to buy milk every day, the ongoing mission will be to reinforce and grow the strength of the brand and its perception of consistent value every day. If on the other hand, you only expect to sell someone something every 20 years, the orientation will be very different, and might instead focus on cross-selling other products or on leveraging social advocacy to create other prospects. Brands or companies with multiple products have their own unique considerations as they think about how to make a customer more valuable over time.

LIFECYCLE STAGES

The value of a customer is a direct result of how well you understand their lifecycle.

One way to look at lifecycle is in terms of sales potential. Most examinations of a customer's lifecycle see it through the lens of the first sale. Custora, for example uses simple classifications for the key stages of their lifecycle: "One and done," "Active," "At risk," and "Lost." This approach helps sales and marketing to focus on appropriate tactics to maximize or mitigate outcomes, in the early stages of the relationship, but it doesn't address long-term lifecycles. Jim Sterne and Matt Cutler in their 2000 paper "E-Metrics, Business Metrics for the New Economy" broke down the customer lifecycle as follows:

1. **Reach**—Marketing outreach to get people's initial attention
2. **Acquisition**—The cultivation stage where you nurture a prospect's interest
3. **Conversion**—Converting interest into sales
4. **Retention**—Keeping clients and selling them more
5. **Loyalty**—Turning customers into advocates and ambassadors

While this includes retention and loyalty, it still looks at the lifecycle in a very linear way. What it misses, which may be because it came out in the very early days of the digital revolution, is the circular repetition that you can see in McKinsey's Consumer Decision Journey. The Sterne Cutler stages are constantly repeated over the life of a customer, and a brand has to get them right every time.

You don't need to be a business person to intuitively understand this, but as we saw in our discussion of the Reach stage in Chapter 3, the Acquisition stage in Chapter 4 and the Conversion stage in Chapter 5, it's often more complex than it appears on the surface.

In a nutshell, the lifecycle challenge is to retain customers, minimize defections and churn, increase the value of those customers over the lifecycle of their relationship with the brand, and then send them out to bring you new prospects.

PLAN WHAT'S NEXT

Design the most effective lifecycle plans for each persona.

Each target segment, and sometimes each individual customer, needs to have a lifecycle plan. This is essentially a plan for how the relationship with a particular customer should develop over time. In financial services, for example, clients may open a relationship in any number of ways. Perhaps someone starts by buying life insurance, or getting a mortgage, or even a car loan. If this new customer is 24, single and just got their first car loan, then perhaps retirement investing might not be the best next subject. If, however, that person is 34, with two small kids and a solid income, then perhaps it might be. The opportunity is to use the behavioral data you gather on all your customers to help design the most effective lifecycle plans for each persona.

Always sell the "right" next thing in order to maximize the potential with a particular customer.

Understanding how you can build a foundation of trust, layer by layer, so that you are always selling the "right" next thing and maximizing the potential of a particular customer, is the job of lifecycle planning. In our work for a big tech company we became aware, at the time, of the siloed nature of each business unit in the company. Each software, hardware and services sub-brand had their own organization and marketing team. Customers, however, were shared, and this resulted in a situation where each brand was running parallel marketing against the same customers without any apparent concern for lifecycle management or the volume of marketing. We couldn't fault the tens of billions in sales they were bringing in, but the lack of the smart, informed marketing that lifecycle planning delivers was a huge missed opportunity.

Like everything else in modern marketing, lifecycle planning is enabled and empowered by data and your organization's ability to predict probable behavior from it. The power of big datasets is to be able to predict behaviors based on the activity of similar people with similar profiles. This is particularly relevant as you try to figure out what you should be talking about with a customer at any particular time.

5. CUSTOMER RETENTION

THE RETENTION EFFECT

Small increases in customer retention result in huge bumps in profitability over time.

General wisdom holds that it costs up to seven times, or more, to acquire versus retain a customer. Furthermore, Fred Reichheld, in the work he did for his book "The Loyalty Effect," showed that small increases in customer retention result in huge bumps in profitability over time. Of course, it makes sense that a happy, satisfied customer will be more likely to spend more, bring more friends to the party and produce more profits.

Long-term relationships with the right customers can have a disproportionate effect on the profitability of a company.

But Reichheld breaks down real numbers and shows how focusing on developing long-term relationships with the right customers can have a disproportionate effect on the profitability of a company over time. In fact, he notes that the longer you keep a customer, the more valuable that customer becomes as the cost of servicing that customer goes down and their loyalty gets stronger.

IDENTIFY PROFITABLE SEGMENTS

Never forget that profit is your ultimate goal.

The right retention strategy starts with identifying those customer segments that have the greatest potential for lifetime value. While it seems like increasing retention for all customers would be a good idea, you'd be surprised how many segments of your customer base actually cost you money or don't deliver much to the bottom line. The old adage that 20% of your customers deliver 80% of your profits is so often true. When you think about how much effort, time and money is poured into the 80% of customers who deliver only 20% of the return, it makes sense to focus your precious resources on those customers that have the most potential. For many companies walking away from any income may seem inconceivable, but once you know what a customer is really worth, it gets easier.

You'd be surprised how many segments of your customer base actually cost you money.

Segmentation of your consumers is critical work that we talked about in Chapter 1. Mapping the potential audience for your brand into segments and then prioritizing those segments is essential before you can start chasing them. It helps concentrate your acquisition dollars on the customers you should really want to have; it also helps you stay focused after those prospects turn into customers. Segmentation is the foundation of your marketing strategy and as such it's critical to ensure it's not out of date, with a minimum bi-annual refresh to make sure it still reflects reality. It's really easy when you're in the thick of day-to-day battle with the pressure of budgets and targets looming over you to sacrifice the quality of the data you rely on to make all your critical decisions…. Don't.

STRATEGIES FOR EACH SEGMENT

The more targeted your strategies, the more effective they will be.

With reliable segmentation in hand and having selected your primary segments based on an analysis of their potential for profitability and growth, you will need a retention strategy for each that is designed to grow their value as customers over time. Hopefully your segments are not too broad, reflect a cohesive life group, and have been turned into personas, as we discussed in Chapter 1. This allows you to craft retention strategies that fit the psychology, lifestyle and unique needs of each segment. Clearly different life-groups have different realities and need retention tactics that are designed for their needs, but there are some basic dynamics that you should always keep in mind.

Craft retention strategies that fit the psychology, lifestyle and needs of each segment.

Three Guiding Strategies:

1. **Know your customer**—Having deep insight into your customer and reflecting that knowledge in every interaction they have with your brand is the foundation for the smart relationships that brands need to have with today's consumers. Communicating this customer orientation, which consumers are looking for, can be as simple as personalization or as sophisticated as recognizing their behavior patterns and responding with something that will surprise and delight them. This could be a room upgrade for the tired traveler after a long day, or a reward for reading ten issues of a newsletter. The key is that it should be clearly personalized to the specific person's behavior. Thanking someone with a discount for being a customer for a year is far more powerful than just giving them one for no apparent reason. Of course, this requires pretty sophisticated systems that can connect the behavioral data dots.

2. **Reward their loyalty**—We will talk more about loyalty programs in a moment, but let's consider the basic idea first. If you go to the same coffee shop every morning and you're greeted by name, it will make it a more personal, meaningful experience. But if you're given a free blueberry muffin because they recognize that you're a regular it will make you feel very special and, of course, even more loyal. This kind of thing happens

organically every day in good companies. The goal is to make it not only part of your culture, but also to cement it into your customer development process, without losing that organic feel.

3. **Make their lives better**—Let's assume that there's more than one coffee shop with great coffee at a reasonable price on your way to work. Let's also assume that they all have nice baristas who might give you a free muffin every now and then. How else can one of them differentiate their brand? This is where utility, especially digital utility, can be very effective. People lead very busy, pressured lives and the digital age has compressed time and forced us all to multi-task, squeezing more productivity out of every moment. So, find out how to make your customers' lives easier and more productive. Starbucks allows you to order your coffee on the way to work with an app and pick it up at the window, saving precious minutes. Plus, the app makes it easier to pay, and automatically enters you for a free coffee with every 12 purchases. Just like an Uber taxi ride, the product is basically the same, but they have made the process easier and, as a result, your life better. But there's no need to stop at utility connected to your product. Starbucks also provides value associated with the lifestyle of their customers by, among other things, offering the music they play in their stores in their app and even letting customers help program their playlists.

These three strategies lead to lots of retention tactics. These will vary as much as products and consumers do, but as you are designing and executing retention tactics, it's also important to remember the new rules of behavior for brand/consumer relationships today.

The New Rules of Brand Behavior

1. **Stay in sync**—in any kind of relationship, if the other side has the wrong expectations, there will be trouble. Aligning expectations should be a constant process from the outset, so that confusion and disappointment can be minimized. Consumers are often moving fast and not paying enough attention to the details. It's an essential marketing truth that your customer communications are way more important to you than to your target consumers. Don't expect them to pay the same attention to detail that you do. That's why when a problem happens that is their fault, you can lose a customer anyway if you blame them and don't quickly help them solve it.

2. **Listen and hear**—The old way was for brands to just talk, talk, talk. Now consumers expect to be listened to. But if you don't show that you have also heard, and then respond to them with some confirmation or

action, then they will conclude that your listening is just empty posturing and more marketing BS.

3. **Talk back and celebrate**—There is nothing wrong with talking to your customers. Just don't be the guy at the party who only talks about himself. How boring is that? Your customers don't mind a brand talking about itself, but only if it's about things that they are interested in, which is something you should know. A good practice is to remind customers about previous purchases that presumably have made them happy in the past. This will reinforce why they liked your brand in the first place and the good experiences they have had with you. It may buy a brand a little more tolerance for the sales messages they often can't wait to fire off.

4. **Create a personalized vision**—If you want a customer to take a journey with you, tell them where they are going and why. Articulate the journey and then guide them step by step. If you are off to see the Wizard, show them an image of Oz in the distance and the yellow brick road that will take them there. It helps. Let's say you are in the home automation business. Give your customer a vision for what their perfect automated home could be like. Then make it their goal too, and help them, step by step, to achieve it. Making the complex easy always buys you gratitude and trust.

5. **Be consistent across channels**—Make sure your brand experience in every interaction, regardless of channel, is consistent, and what you want it to be. You do this when you are trying to acquire people, so make sure you continue to do it with all your customer interactions. Think of it as a growing friendship; the last thing you want to be is the inconsistent, unreliable friend.

6. **Connect the dots**—Make sure the left hand knows what the right hand is doing and *has* done. This speaks to being fully informed by data. The more sophisticated you can make this the better. But it starts with something as simple as making sure a telephone agent has the customer's file on their screen when that same customer has just punched it into their phone. How frustrating is it when you are put through hoops for no apparent reason? What does it say about a company when you give them your ID and then they deliver you to someone who asks for your ID? Connecting the dots extends to your ERP system, which needs to inform your CRM system every time a customer buys something or takes a significant action. This should also cross-pollinate information with your marketing MAP system and the software (CMS) that runs the content on your website and apps. Working together these systems can deliver individually relevant,

personalized experiences for your customers, which is what they expect.

7. **Give to get**—Give away content and anything thing else that can be of value to your customers. Giving content, knowledge and help, before you get something in return, is an act of trust and faith that consistently delivers results. Not only will it attract exactly the people you are looking for through search and social media, but there seems to be a human need to reciprocate generosity and trust. Brands can spark a virtuous cycle of giving by showing their customers a little generosity up front.

8. **Be people not the Borg**—Over the years Star Trek has had a number of episodes that featured an alien race called the Borg, made up of drones executing the directions of the collective "hive" mind. Needless to say, people are not fond of Borg-like organizations, so don't be one. Create an internal culture that presents itself as people: individuals who care, and with whom your customers can create bonds and relationships. Every time you have a good experience with a person who behaves like a human being, you want to have the opportunity to continue and build on that relationship. However, all too often companies miss a huge opportunity by making it impossible to ever speak to that same person again.

6. CUSTOMER SERVICE

THE HIDDEN COST

> The Customer Service department should be renamed the Customer Opportunity department.

Customer service is so much more than it used to be. We used to think of it as the complaint department where people went with their problems. We knew that for every customer who complained there were always many more who might feel the same way, but who didn't make the effort. Since they would only tell a couple of friends, the thinking went, it had minimal effect. Now, however, with virtually no effort, consumers can share their feelings with hundreds and even thousands of people instantly.

> With a click, the average person can unleash their influence with over 155 friends on Facebook alone.

Consumer power to influence the perception of a brand on social media is, therefore, huge, not only with friends, and friends of friends, but with people all over the internet who may discover their opinions through search. This creates a very different customer service calculation for brands. Now the cost of not fixing a $5 problem may be many thousands of dollars.

THE POINT OF THE SPEAR

Every consumer interaction is a chance to influence opinions about your brand.

That starts, of course, with making disgruntled customers happy whenever possible as part of a consumer-oriented brand culture in which customers are cherished. Similarly, every functional interaction, from digital channels to shipping, becomes a metaphor for the brand's attitude about their customers and should be a chance for its customer service culture to score a win. This requires a level of sensitivity to consumer perceptions and feelings that brands have never needed before, and which should inform all policies, processes, systems, and culture.

Every employee who engages with consumers is the point of the spear and can have a profound effect on the health of the brand.

This work starts with the process we identified in Chapter 1, which seeks to understand the psychology of buyers and customers and which should be used to guide how a company responds in each situation. While these qualitative elements will shape how a brand is perceived by its customers and will in turn have a great effect on retention, there are also a number of mechanical things to get right.

CONNECTING

People forget the details of an interaction, but they remember how it made them feel.

The simple act of reaching out to a brand should be easy and delightful, yet how many companies make this happen? Since we are all consumers ourselves, most of us can agree that the experience of communicating with many companies is frequently disappointing and often even damaging to the perception we have of their brand.

The experience of connecting with a company is a reflection of how much they value their customers.

Calling a company, for example, should be easy. You should not have to wade through endless decision trees, and you should not be made to wait (an experience which communicates how little a brand values your time, and by extension, you). You should receive an email confirmation of the call and the actions that will ensue, and you should be able to talk to the same person again or failing that have an incident number to use if you need to follow up. Reps should also get the caller's telephone number, so they can call back in case they are cut off. The opportunity to talk to your customer is a rare and precious opportunity. This is not the time or the place to save money. This is a chance to make a powerful impression and cement a relationship.

DON'T HIDE

Customer service is not the place to cut corners.

In digital channels, the email address and other contact information, including telephone numbers, should be prominently displayed. Yes, customer service is expensive, but hiding contact information is a very short-sighted way to try to reduce cost. Response times to email should be fast, and for those that want answers immediately, brands should also have Twitter staffed, as well as online chat, which should be quick and responsive, as opposed to one agent trying to field a hundred conversations. The point is that corners cut in customer service cost much more than they save in the long run.

The simpler, faster and more responsive customer service is, the more a brand will be perceived as customer-oriented.

As digitally enabled customers become more and more discerning in their brand choices, especially in parity categories, customer service becomes a meaningful proxy for the nature of their entire relationship with a brand and will directly affect retention. Customer service can win the enthusiastic loyalty of a customer or quickly lose it. The calculation for companies should be to maximize the positive effects that customer service can have on the brand and use every interaction as an opportunity to create beneficial waves that ripple through the social media waters.

7. DATA INTEGRATION

CONNECTING THE DOTS

The cost of an integrated system is less than the cost of not having one.

Consumers expect brands to know what's going on in their world. They don't care how complicated it might be for companies; they want a brand to act like a person who doesn't forget you and remembers what you've said or done in the past.

Consumers want brands to deliver the experience they want, and like a great entertainer, they want it to look effortless.

Winston Churchill was one of the greatest orators in history, and also one of the cleverest debaters. But his formidable wit, like his legendary speeches, was the product of hours of writing, practice, and rehearsal. The point is, the effortless experience that consumers want takes the hard work of developing top-notch integrated systems. Your call centers need information about the customers they are talking to. Those interactions also create valuable information that needs to inform your marketing, retention and lifecycle tactics as well as your overall strategies. Similarly, your other interaction channels from brick-and-mortar stores to email, snail mail, your website, and mobile apps, require data from other parts of your ecosystem and produce essential data that will be needed elsewhere. As technology has shifted consumer expectations to a higher bar, brands must invest in the systems and strategies to connect the dots.

CONSUMER EXPECTATIONS

When customer experience is a priority companies out perform their competition.

Only with comprehensive systems integration can a company and its brands behave the way consumers want and expect. While this is still comparatively rare in small companies, the technology to integrate systems is starting to proliferate and become affordable for midsized companies. Since many consumers have already enjoyed these experiences from large companies, they are coming to expect it from all companies and are disappointed and even aggravated when they don't get it.

Consumers want a company focused on them and their needs, and they don't care how hard it is.

The integration that companies should aspire to starts with the connection of sales and customer data coming from POS (point-of-sale) and ERP (enterprise resource management), with CRM (customer relationship management) systems. This will enable individualized marketing and sales communications, such as email, to be personally customized and relevant to customers, and should inform CMS (content management systems) which control what content appears, where, on brand websites and mobile apps. It also includes MAP (marketing automation platforms), which are increasingly integrated with CRM, to enable sales and marketing activities to be fully informed by customer data and activity. The result is a smooth, effortless customer experience where the website knows you and only presents what is relevant; phone reps have your information at their fingertips, emails are only about stuff you are interested in, and your mobile app reflects your history. No wasted time. No annoying, irrelevant sales pitches. Just a company that knows you and is focused on your needs.

8. ADVOCACY

THE POWER OF REFERRALS

According to Nielson 92% of consumers trust referrals from people they know.

A few other stats about referrals:

- People are four times more likely to buy when referred by a friend—*Nielsen*
- 77% of consumers are more likely to buy a new product when learning about it from friends or family—*Nielsen*
- 81% of U.S. online consumers' purchase decisions are influenced by their friends' social media posts—*Market Force*
- 74% of consumers identify word-of-mouth as a key influencer in their purchasing decision—*Ogilvy/Google/TNS*
- 58% of consumers share their positive experiences with a company and ask family, colleagues, and friends for their opinions about brands.—*SDL*

The above, part of a comprehensive list compiled by Social Annex, was actually over 80 stats, each more powerful than the last. It makes clear the point that social media influence and the social power of individuals to determine the fate of a brand has become critical to any business. People sharing their happiness, delight and satisfaction not only with their friends, but potentially with everyone on the internet, is free marketing for brands that get it. And not just any marketing, it's the most credible, powerful marketing that exists. That's why brands should want as many advocates as possible.

The objective is to get as many consumer advocates for a brand or product as possible.

Converting customers to advocates begins with giving them a product and service to be excited about. That is harder than ever before because flawed or second-rate brands and products have few places to hide from the reach of social media. The difficult fact is that the social internet illuminates every inadequacy of a product or brand so mercilessly that the foundation of all success, from this point on, will always be the inherent excellence of what you are selling. While Apple has always had good marketing, the philosophy behind it has always been to have the best products; so good they don't really need any marketing.

ACTIVATING CUSTOMERS

Your best customers are usually your best advocates for new prospects.

Assuming that you have a strong product and brand, how do you encourage your customers to become advocates? There are many ways, from simply asking for a review after every transaction, to enabling the creation of consumer-generated content, which can then travel the web on your behalf. In every instance, the idea is to have your customers express themselves and for the brand to feel confident enough to allow that expression to be unencumbered by any attempts at censorship. Unfortunately, the history of social media is littered with brands that refused to enable their customers to voice their opinions, only to see those opinions surface elsewhere as well as brands that tried to manipulate social media and got caught. In both instances, the absence of transparency and honesty revealed not only their lack of confidence in their products and customers, but also their ethical weakness—the kiss of death with today's consumer. For confident brands, ratings and reviews are powerful social proof points, as long as they appear to be credible.

The modus operandi must be the open, transparent enablement of customers and their opinions.

Regardless of your efforts, not all of your customers are advocates, or can become them. That's why it's important to focus on people who are worth your time. Frequent customers, especially those who have been customers for some time, are clear targets. Your list can be further refined by studying feedback such as Net Promoter Scores (NPS), which will identify your best fans. These potential ambassadors then need to be enticed through attention, flattery and rewards to advocate on your behalf, not only to their friends, but also to the world in general. Design a special program which makes them feel a cut above, with perks, incentives and activity goals. You may even want to consider asking them to pay for special privileges or values. Fees for special clubs or privileges work: just ask the people who run Amazon Prime.

9. LOYALTY

THE REAL VALUE

The power of consumer data from multiple sources is growing quickly.

Loyalty programs have evolved, but it's important to be clear about their mission. It should not be blanket retention, or repeat business for its own sake, but rather the retention and growth of profitable customers.

Loyalty programs are far from new; they have been around since supermarkets gave out S&H Green Stamps in the '50s. But they really began to take off with the airlines in the 1980s. Since then, Americans have loaded up on loyalty programs, but not on loyalty itself. Today the average family is signed up for dozens of programs, although they only actively participate in a few. The result is that discerning consumers are well educated in the different program types: points programs, discounts or experience programs. This leads to a level of sophistication about loyalty programs whereby it's no longer enough to just tack on a loyalty program, award points and then expect excited customers to flock to your brand.

Consumer expectations have evolved as have company goals for loyalty programs. Today, for example, the accumulation of customer data and insights is proving to be even more valuable than simple repeat business. Supermarkets, with their rewards programs, not only earn a greater share of wallet from their regular customers but accumulate enormous amounts of data. This data informs marketing strategies and enables supermarkets to charge hefty participation fees to their suppliers, based on the purchasing dynamics of their products.

> The proliferation of rewards programs has made these programs a commodity and led to an entitlement mindset with consumers.

This is happening in the context of a shifting competitive battlefield, where parity products in many verticals are moving the focus from price and product advantages to less tangible and often more loosely associated emotional differentiators. As a result, programs are starting to concentrate more on brand and experience values that capture the attention and imagination of their members.

PART OF THE JOURNEY

> Developing customers after the sale should get as much attention as acquiring them.

Just as we now look at the customer journey as a circle, we should look at loyalty and loyalty programs as another part of that journey. Loyalty takes the customer journey and loops it back to repeat the explore, evaluate and purchase steps in the process, adding in the additional dimension of advocacy. This has made the strategic process, described in Chapter 1 and Chapter 2, all the more important.

> A loyalty program is in many ways a separate brand and, as such, will need to develop its own branding and strategy.

For loyalty programs to work they need to undergo the same rigorous strategy and branding process we outlined for acquisition. Many of the steps that a brand will have already taken in the creation of their overarching strategic process will apply, so it's not like starting from scratch. At IQ, our work with the Intercontinental Hotels Group Rewards program, the largest of its kind in the world, revealed how their awards program, while an extension of their brands, had its own unique strategic and branding dynamics. For example, the success of the program in enticing business travelers to accumulate points, forced us, much of the time, to find ways to entice members to spend those points. Successful programs have their own realities, which are not the same as those of the brand itself, as in this case, where a mountain of unused points represented a large financial liability that needed to be constantly whittled down. Other consider-ations include, for example, how tightly entwined brand perceptions become with the operation of a loyalty program. Airlines are constantly walking a tight-rope with their best customers every time they modify their loyalty programs, always running the danger of alienating one group in the service of another.

STARTING OUT

Instant gratification is becoming an expectation.

Companies just embarking on a loyalty program need to keep abreast of changes that are afoot, not only with loyalty systems and the associated soft-ware, but with consumer psychology. The trend toward giving your best cus-tomers special perks will continue as companies increasingly use experiences to differentiate themselves. Unfortunately, however, while many companies think their loyalty programs are unique, it appears their customers don't agree. In a recent study a majority of retailers, for example, said their programs were unique, but nearly half of their customers said they are interchangeable.

Earning value instantly makes delayed gratification all the more unattractive.

With *experience* being the new battleground, brands are looking for ways, especially in retail and in e-commerce, to enhance customer experience with instant gratification, although it may ultimately turn out to be a self-defeating trap for the brands that indulge in it. But the removal of barriers to instant happiness is a general trend across categories. This will especially be true with the increasing integration of mobile into retail, enabling new ways to bring loyalty to life at the point of sale.

THE BIG VIEW

Getting all the little stuff consistently right will get the big stuff done.

As companies learn how to gather more and more data on their customers, integrated systems that can squeeze segment and individual insights out of behavioral data will start to be the tail that wags the dog. These systems make possible highly targeted loyalty programs with very personalized value. This will enable companies to focus time, money and energy on their most potentially profitable customers. It will also allow for a more comprehensive view of the customer, enabling companies to project their customers' most likely needs and hot buttons throughout their lifecycle. It's this big view of the customer—of their behavior and attitudes—that should guide not only how companies approach loyalty and loyalty programs, but also how they construct their whole consumer experience.

The complexity of getting so many small things consistently right takes a tightly organized, consumer-centric organization.

The line between being a prospect and being a customer has blurred so much that organizations need to have integrated systems, processes and communications informed by a constant stream of behavioral data. The trick, of course, is to make sure that the data is reliable, that your organization is set up to understand it, and is ready to act on it. On paper this might seem obvious, but in practice the complexity of getting so many small things consistently right takes a tightly organized, consumer-centric organization that is equipped, focused and empowered by management with a strategic vision that guides the way.

CHAPTER 7

FIRING ON ALL CYLINDERS

How to build and operate the system

EXECUTIVE SUMMARY

Deciding to do something is usually much easier than getting it done. Most executives realize they need to put the strategies, policies, technology and people in place to make their company consumer-centric, but getting that accomplished often challenges the status quo and inertia at work in many companies. This chapter talks about how to get your modern marketing system built. It then goes on to discuss what it takes to make sure that the system is operating at its maximum potential.

Technology & People

- Today, brands can build and own a self-sustaining brand marketing system.
- Most of the tech pieces are readily accessible.
- Getting your system built requires organizational support.
- Getting the right people to run it is still a challenge.

Infrastructure

- The objective is to have a consumer-centric organization that delivers the best consumer experience possible.
- This requires marketing technology that becomes the infrastructure of the system.
- It makes sense to invest in repeatable marketing infrastructure versus one-time paid media.
- Brands that get a system up and running can still get big competitive advantages.

Planning

- With the rise of cloud-based solutions, it is easier, faster, and cheaper to install and adapt system software.
- The battlefield is already shifting from who has the software to what brands are doing with it.
- Strategy and ideation are now the keys to success.

Requirements

- You need the understanding, buy-in and compliance of employees to get your system up and working.
- The bulk of the choices involved will be business evaluations, and should be made by marketing versus IT.
- Get key stakeholder support by getting them involved from the outset.
- Leadership needs to present a clear vision and rationale for the project.

Picking Your Team

- Marketing systems are just digital junk without the vision and creativity of a good team.
- Decide which roles should be on the internal team versus outsourced.
- This mix of in-house and out-of-house resources is a key strategic decision.

Agencies

- Brands and companies turn to agencies for fresh, out-of-the-box thinking.
- Agencies provide a broad range of marketing and technology expertise.
- You need to perfectly align your needs with the capabilities and experience of an agency.
- Selecting an agency is difficult.

Content

- Content is part of every consideration.
- Your brand will be judged by the relevance, quality, and originality of your content.
- The strategic work, which tells you what content to make and why, is critical.
- Creative talent and experience are still the way to excellence.

Consumer-Centricity

- Put the consumer at the center of everything.
- Anyone who interacts with consumers on behalf of your company is key.
- Show your people how what they do fits into the plan; they will support it.
- Changing to a consumer orientation may upset many long-standing modus operandi.

---

1. TECHNOLOGY & PEOPLE

JUST DO IT

Technology enables brands to build their own proprietary marketing systems.

Digital technology has not only created direct channels between companies and consumers, it has also reshaped how the marketplace works. Today, brands can build and own their own self-sustaining brand marketing systems. This means that instead of the bulk of marketing dollars going to pay others for short-term results, brands can now invest in their own marketing infrastructure and get long-term returns. The tough part is not deciding the system should be built but getting everyone committed to the hard work of getting it done.

The tech pieces of the system are more accessible than ever, but getting the right people is still a challenge.

Throughout this book we have discussed what this consumer-centric marketing system should look like, and the technology and software that is needed to power it. This technology is, of course, changing and evolving all the time, and, like any technology, requires constant attention. But with few exceptions, most of the tech pieces are readily accessible. It's still a challenge, of course, to introduce new ways of doing things to any organization, but companies that are tackling this essential work are primed to reap the rewards. Driving this are consumers who expect very high levels of integrated experience and don't care about how hard it might be to do. While sitting out these changes and investments might have been an option in and around the recession, today there is nowhere for companies to hide from demanding consumer expectations.

Just building this integrated consumer experience system, however, is not enough. In the '80s, many companies became enamored with the possibilities that satellite technology gave them to communicate with their offices and customers around the world. As a result, they were persuaded to install costly TV studios and satellite technology. Before long, these major investments gathered dust as companies struggled to understand how to operate them. The lesson was that just buying technology isn't worth anything unless you are prepared to invest in smart operations. A marketing system is like a car: it needs fuel, maintenance, navigation and good drivers.

2. INFRASTRUCTURE

THE GIFT THAT GOES ON GIVING

A well-designed, integrated system will deliver value for many years.

The days of brands manipulating consumers are gone. Today, the challenge is to have genuinely superior products and a consumer-centric organization that provides the smoothest, most satisfying experience possible. Whereas marketers used to focus on the message of the moment, now they need to entice consumers with real value at every turn. That's why companies need to invest in best-in-class systems that connect the dots in all channels from retail to digital and customer service. Everything the consumer sees or touches that could possibly reflect the brand needs to provide a consistently smart, customer-centric experience. This requires marketing technology that becomes the infrastructure that frames the system.

Invest in repeatable marketing infrastructure versus one-time paid media.

When data is flowing properly between the integrated acronym soup of POS, ERP, CRM, CMS and MAP systems, the job then becomes to focus on the strategies, tactics and content that fuel and activate the whole machine. Today's marketing technology is pretty remarkable, and brands that harness its power can rise to the next level. It is not yet, however, super easy to put the pieces together and operate these systems, which is why brands that master these new disciplines now can still get big competitive advantages.

3. PLANNING

BUILD IT, AND THEY WILL COME

New cloud-based solutions are easier, cheaper and faster to implement.

Like building a town, you need a plan, so everything is in harmony when it's all done. While often charming, cities that have developed organically over time are rarely functional compared to planned cities. The problem is that each piece of the marketing city you are building is still a major investment in time and effort, and there are a number of pieces that you will need before everything is finished. Often brands tend to focus on the piece that is causing the most immediate pain, like putting in a CRM system to support sales, when they should be looking at the bigger picture. Each of these pieces will ultimately need to work together and that requirement shapes how every piece should be configured.

Planning a marketing system is like urban planning. When your city is built, you want everything to work together.

Selecting the right solution for each part of the puzzle is a complex, time-consuming business, especially with so many options to consider. The good news is that with the rise of cloud-based solutions, which are easier to adopt, install, and adapt, companies can get set up much more quickly with far less cost and risk than before. In recent years each of the big categories of marketing software, CRM, CMS, and MAP have become better, cheaper and more accessible for smaller companies. Now the software industry is focusing their attention on simplifying integration so that everything can work together seamlessly.

These technologies affect how you set up and manage many of the elements of your marketing system. The following is a list of the more common elements, many of which have been discussed in previous chapters. Each of these pieces will be powered by one or more of the software types listed above.

Primary brand ecosystem elements:

- **Brand website**

  We have talked elsewhere about your brand site but suffice to say this is usually a big deal, as it should be. In a modern brand ecosystem, the brand site is the beating heart of the whole enterprise. It's much more than the online brochure of old. Today's brand site should be able to make a personalized pitch for all your products, manage the sales process, attract searchers, identify prospects, close deals, service existing customers, job applicants, investors and press, and enhance the brand. Done well, your brand site will be your most valuable marketing asset.

  Sites need to be planned very carefully; in fact, this is actually where a large portion of your website cost should go. This planning includes detailed work to figure out what the site needs to accomplish, why and when—especially for prospects. You need to be clear about how it will be managed, what functionality it requires, from e-commerce to content, and what data analytics you want.

  Building a brand website is a classic case of "you get what you pay for." Brochure websites can cost as little as $9 a month, but websites that need to generate millions of dollars, and act as marketing hubs, need much more. While many might imagine that building a website is about technology and design, that is actually the easy part today. Much of the cost goes into two areas that the less experienced may not be thinking much about: strategy and content. It's the strategic thinking and content of a site that makes it work or not. Good technology and design are table stakes and not where the game is won or lost today, as it once was.

It is also important to note that the creation of a brand website has become much more of a marketing than technology exercise. Solid technology is still vital, of course, but while the IT department used to run the whole process and saw it through a fairly narrow IT lens, this leadership has now correctly shifted to the marketing team. This is in recognition that the brand website is first and foremost serving a marketing mission, and that the required technology is much more plug-and-play, and readily accessible. In days past building a website required a great deal of custom coding by engineers. In contrast, today the technology required is often in the form of modules that you choose from a menu of options.

The CMS will be the most important technology for your site, and one of your biggest technology decisions. MAP will also need to be integrated, hopefully already connected to a CRM system. Additionally, sites will need analytics software, and potentially other software capabilities, such as ratings and reviews, chat, e-commerce, internal search, and more.

- **Social websites**

A brand's social media presence is, as previously noted, critical. This requires not only the creation and management of social media sites such as on Facebook, but also the creation of a constant stream of relevant and compelling content. As with many things in our maturing digital world, the technology component has become relatively straightforward and off the shelf, while the battle has moved to strategy, content, ideas, and their execution.

- **Mobile apps & sites**

Mobile continues to occupy more and more of the marketing landscape as the technology and consumer adoption mature. But there is still a way to go until brand mobile sites and apps give consumers the ease and flexibility they want. Mobile technology is now more easily accessible to brands, which means getting apps built is becoming cheaper, faster and easier. But ensuring that the value the apps presents to the consumer is meaningful, and that the user experience will be valuable, is no easier than it has ever been. It's important to note that apps are not always the answer. Sometimes a mobile site makes more sense, and sometimes the smartest thing is not to do anything. Of course, the technology continues to evolve, but already the challenge is what goes in the mobile channel, rather than building the channel itself.

- **Blogs, etc.**
  As with so many digital vehicles, creating blogs and podcasts is easy now, at least technically. The challenge is determining why the content in the blog will command anyone's time and attention, and how to make it compelling.

- **Customer service**
  How a brand handles customer relationships has always been important. Today with sky-high consumer expectations it has become a critical element of success. Whether it's data feeding into your CS reps, chat applications, or managing outsourced services, the good news is that software and innovative support services make many of the CS elements that companies need for a world-class offering readily available. The job, however, is not just checking the boxes to make sure you have all the requisite pieces, but rather to connect them in a way that is the right reflection of the brand, and which super-serves the expectations of your customers.

- **Analytics**
  Analytics is the business of understanding the impact of what your brand is doing so that you can quickly adjust and improve. With the reams of data that all our consumer interactions and systems produce, brands need effective tools to quickly understand it all. The idea is to get meaningful, actionable insights as fast as possible and then respond to those insights in a way that impacts performance. Insights are often time-sensitive, and if you wait their value will fade. Analytics is equal parts technology and human analysis. You need sophisticated systems to measure the right metrics, in the right way, and then you need to quickly turn those numbers into insights you can use. This is first made possible by software that gathers data, looks at trends and presents them in easy to understand ways. This then enables analysts and strategists to spot insights, which become the launch pad for ideas designed to solve problems, take advantage of opportunities, or propel your brand to the next level.

  Anything that produces data can be measured and can contribute to an understanding of consumer behavior. ERP and POS systems produce and store customer sales data, CRM produces customer behavior data, as does MAP software. Activity in websites, apps, social media, email, and texts communications also contribute pieces of the behavior puzzle. Other software measures social media sentiment as well as social media activity. This data can reveal different types of insights from the small, at the individual level, to the very large, at the data-set level.

There are a number of suppliers of comprehensive data analytics packages, such as Adobe. They measure everything from advertising effectiveness and website performance to sales. These packages are not inexpensive, and companies are often tempted to forego the cost and use cheaper offerings, such as Google analytics. However, this route invariably gives the enterprise much less actionable data and results in a marketing culture that is less focused on insights and metrics. This can shift a marketing team's focus away from the incremental improvements that contribute to a superior performance and can result in a reliance on old school, gut decision-making, which is increasingly a dead end in our complex world.

- **Email**
  As discussed elsewhere, email is an enormously valuable marketing tool if used correctly. Email requires sophisticated segmentation and content strategies, but the technology is mature, inexpensive, and readily available. It is important to ensure that it seamlessly integrates with all your other technologies and user experience. This leads brands to increasingly use email capabilities already built into CRM or MAP software, or to work with platforms that have easily implemented APIs, which integrate systems together.

- **Retail**
  Kiosks, digital display and beacons are just a few of many ways that marketers are using to extend their marketing systems into retail locations. But the technologies are always changing, succeeding, or failing. As consumer behavior at retail evolves, so does the technology to influence it. Dozens of technologies are being tested in retail, including location-specific, text-broadcasting systems designed to deliver messages to customers in store. As consumers increasingly use their phones in stores to price check and consult reviews, companies are devising ways to influence this final step in the journey leveraging the ever-present smart phone.

- **Marketing team enablement**
  Organizations must produce a great deal of marketing content to fuel their brand system, and they need tools to help them. This includes Digital Asset Management (DAM) software, which makes the process of cataloging, storing, accessing, and distributing marketing content such as images, designs, posts, and ads, much easier and more reliable. Other tools include the creative toolsets and process integration tools available from Adobe, Microsoft, and others, which enable creative and marketing teams to rapidly produce, share, and distribute work. Not long ago, for example, if you needed to

make a change to your website you had to use a software engineer to get it done. Now, most modern marketing technologies are designed to be operated by non-technical staff, which makes getting work done faster and cheaper.

- **CRM**

  Customer relationship management software, such as Salesforce, is in use by many companies. While many think of it as sales enablement, most CRM packages are designed to facilitate an informed, automated relationship with customers based on historical data. This can incorporate service and sales needs. Any company that has more customers than their sales and service people can individually reach out and touch must use some kind of CRM system in order to manage the day-to-day communications that good marketing and customer service requires. This is a critical link in the value chain, where customers have come to expect that the companies they do business with know them and the history of their interactions with the company. Salesforce, and other CRM software, helps accomplish that by keeping all the data associated with a customer attached to that customer's record. This can then be accessed by salespeople or marketers through alerts triggered by the activity or profile of the individual customer. As consumer expectations continue to rise, the only way to ensure consistent, well-informed, relevant communications is with software that does it automatically.

- **MAP**

  Marketing automation platforms (MAP) enable companies to track the behavior of both prospects and customers in digital channels. They monitor the activity of consumers on websites, mobile, email, and social media, and enable marketers to track prospects and customers. They then automate marketing communications to them through the various stages of their journey. For sales, they identify hot prospects, based on their behavior, and when the activity of the prospect rises to a set threshold, identify them for personal follow-up. Increasingly, CRM companies are integrating their software with MAP systems, which they are building or acquiring, such as Pardot, acquired by Salesforce.

- **CMS**

  Content Management Systems were originally conceived of as systems that enabled companies to easily make changes to their website. They made it simple for non-technical employees to update content without getting web developers involved. They also made it easy for organizations to make numerous changes across a website at the same time, such as updating a logo on every page. Instead of having to custom code changes to the site, a CMS gives the marketing team an intuitive, user-friendly interface, eliminating the need for specially trained staff. Today, however, CMS software goes much further, and through integration with other databases, enables brand websites to deliver personalized content experiences to viewers in real time. This means that a website can automatically present content that is designed to appeal to a specific individual. The result is a website experience that is personally relevant and much more compelling. The powerful combination of a CMS system integrated with CRM and MAP lets brands deliver content designed to cultivate, upsell, and cross-sell customers based on history and behavior.

Software tools make it easier to deliver content and messaging to prospects and customers at exactly the right moment, and every day they are getting easier to use and integrate with other systems. These technologies have already been fully implemented by large companies and now are being rapidly adopted by smaller companies. The result is that the battlefield is shifting from who has the software to what brands are doing with it. For a long time, it was enough for companies to be the first to deploy a new technology, but we have now reached the stage when ideas and execution are the keys to success.

4. REQUIREMENTS

THE RIGHT TOOLS

The hard work of making smart choices is worth it.

The objective is to use technology to handle the mechanics and free your team to focus on consumer engagement. Hopefully, the power of an integrated system to do this is clear by now. Now come the questions of which technology systems to get, what you want them to do, and how to set up your organization to execute. This is usually a much bigger challenge than making the decision to invest in the first place.

The challenge invariably is getting the system built and then making sure it lives up to its potential.

But these are not the only solutions you will have to craft. Invariably new systems require different ways of working. This often means changes to workflow, processes, command structures, compliance, reporting, and more. In other words, they require big changes to how your organization does things. That's why you will need the understanding, buy-in and compliance of employees if your new systems are going to work. This list of hills to be climbed may be daunting, but they shouldn't prevent companies from working to put these essential marketing systems in place. Without them, any company's ability to compete on the modern stage will be greatly reduced.

INPUT

Getting buy-in from your key people is critical for success.

Like all good planning, the job is to make sure that you have considered everything carefully before jumping ahead. You need to seek out all points of view with the goal of understanding what your systems will need to accomplish. You also need to understand what is possible with each element of the system. This requires not only evaluating different offerings in each software category, but also analyzing their relative strengths and weaknesses. Even though these are technical systems, in that they are software, the bulk of these key choices will be business decisions and, as such, should be guided by business and marketing people. This is not to say that the input and consultation of IT is not important. Instead it's reflective of how the role of technology has changed as it has evolved.

The best place to start is with your key discipline leaders.

Having sketched out the way an integrated marketing system can work with CRM, MAP, CMS and other types of software working together, you need to hear from the people who will be most responsible for using it. Like every human endeavor, it is essential to get the key stakeholders to support the plan, and the best way to do that is to have them involved from the outset. Start with a key leader workshop, which lays the groundwork for the design and functional specifications of each piece of the integrated system you are building. If people are involved in the design of the system and feel they are listened to, they will be much more likely to make sure it succeeds. With this outline in place, and the buy-in of the leadership team, you can also start to consider how new systems and processes might change workflows and responsibilities. This will become critical to success. Many of us have seen instances where the quiet refusal of one group to implement even one step in a process can undermine an entire new system.

CLEAR VISION

Senior leadership needs to visibly sponsor and promote the initiative.

Change is hard for any organization, so mapping the timetable, process and responsibilities for everyone involved from kick-off through roll-out is essential. Everyone needs to know what their job is, what is expected of them, what they need to deliver, and when. Clearly, an initiative of this importance will need its own leader and team, to hold people accountable for their piece of the puzzle. Stakeholders and employees need to understand not only how this system will affect them, but more importantly, how it will enable the company to achieve its greater goals. To that end, senior leadership needs to visibly sponsor and promote the initiative and take the responsibility of explaining to the organization why it is being done.

The most important job of the leadership is to present a clear vision for what the entire project will accomplish.

Much as we would all like to go through the process of evaluating and selecting products as fast and easily as possible, there really is no shortcut to doing it right. That's made harder when in all likelihood everyone still has to keep doing their regular jobs. The approach is, therefore, to design the evaluation of vendors based on functional requirements that you have already agreed upon internally. It is then a straightforward process of requiring vendors to respond with the specific information that you need in order to produce valid apple-to-apple comparisons.

Software vendors are usually helpful in this, and as long as your process is objective and consistent, you will likely get to a good recommendation. With a short list of companies that make the grade in each category, it is then always a good idea to talk to their current and past customers. This is where consultants like Forrester and Gartner, can provide reliable shortcuts with objective product performance research. Gartner, for example, produces their Magic Quadrant analysis for almost every critical software category. This allows companies to evaluate offerings based on their strengths and weaknesses quickly and easily.

5. PICKING YOUR TEAM

THE RIGHT STUFF

When everyone has the systems in place people will make the difference.

The marketing system you are building with its various pieces of interconnected software will allow your team to be brilliant, to respond quickly to changing market conditions, and to be laser-focused on consumers, but it will not do their jobs for them. The challenge rapidly becomes to take full advantage of the awesome power of all the technology you've invested in, and that takes a talented, motivated team. This can be a completely internal marketing team, a completely outsourced team, or something in between.

While modern marketing systems are amazing, they are just digital junk without the vision, creativity and execution of a good team.

You will need many different types of specialists. This starts with strategists and branding experts. Then you'll need people for all the digital specialties from social media to analytics, a variety of technologies, search, and more. You'll also need writers, designers, photographers, user experience experts, video production teams, media planners, project managers, and the list goes on. Some you'll need full time, some you'll need occasionally, and some you'll only need once. Deciding which of these roles and types of people should be on the internal team versus hired guns are critical decisions.

THE INTERNAL TEAM

Carefully consider what roles should be in-house.

Your internal marketing team will need to be cohesive, motivated, committed to your company and onboard for the long haul. You don't want to hire superstars that you can't and won't keep. They need to have sufficient experience and knowledge to, at minimum, manage outside specialists in each area. They don't have to do everything themselves, but they are ultimately responsible for calling BS on outside vendors, especially in technology. Without knowledge and experience you may be at their mercy. Project management experience is also very useful because so much of the work will be coordinating the work of others. At the same time competition for some of the roles you may be filling, such as creatives, designers and digital developers, can be fierce, with all manner of companies, including tech and agencies, vying for the same people. While finding someone who can write is easy, finding someone who can write well is hard. Therefore, think carefully about the roles that are best suited to having within your organization.

Determining this mix of in-house and out-of-house resources is a key strategic choice by leadership.

If, like many companies, you decide to outsource part or all of your marketing functions, you will need to structure your internal team accordingly. Be sure it is designed to complement your agency rather than duplicate their capabilities. And if you elect to use multiple agencies, you will need to organize your team to coordinate the complexity of multiple organizations.

Another consideration is your size. Very large companies, like the Fortune 100, are increasingly staffing a great deal of marketing internally. This includes their digital teams, from social media to design and technology. These companies often have marketing departments with hundreds of people in them and are essentially in-house agencies. For small- and medium-sized companies with less volume of work, this usually doesn't make sense and agency outsourcing can work. Whichever way you go, however, having the right people on your internal team is as important as having the right systems.

6. AGENCIES

MANY FLAVORS

Understand what kind of agency you will need.

There are many flavors of agencies that help brands and companies with their marketing needs. These range from classic advertising agencies to brand agencies, digital agencies, media agencies and more. There are those that specialize in one thing, such as digital; a category, such as financial services; or even an age group, like millennials. And then there are those that do everything, often called full-service agencies, which means they either do it all themselves, or do the key work and manage other specialist agencies when needed. Finding the perfect partner, or partners, is challenging because you need to perfectly align your needs with the capabilities and experience of an agency. This can be hard if you are not sure what your needs really are.

It can be a daunting task to find and hire exactly the right agency.

To find the right agency you first must understand what you need. This begins with solid business strategy (Chapter 1) that tells you what marketing has to deliver to support your business goals. This then informs the brand and marketing strategy, which tells you what skills and capabilities you will need. It's a bit of a chicken-and-egg situation, because ideally your agency should work with you to produce your brand and marketing strategy. In most situations, companies already understand their needs sufficiently to select a partner who can help take them the rest of the way.

OUTSIDE THE BOX

Disruptive ideas and creativity often needs to come from outside.

Agencies usually have very different cultures than corporate organizations, which is one of the ways they attract and retain people with the right talents. Part of this cultural difference is an iconoclastic attitude, where the objective is often to turn the status quo on its head in the search for new ideas. This is in contrast to many corporate cultures where continuity and consistency versus risk, are highly valued. That's why brands and companies turn to agencies for the fresh, out-of-the-box thinking that it often takes to get consumers to pay attention in a noisy, competitive world.

Working with multiple clients breeds a breadth of experience for many agency people that is rarely possible with the focus on a single brand.

Agency people bring the know-how gained from other brands and categories to bear in solving challenges. When this push for new ideas is married to strategic insight and discipline, agencies can deliver break-through ideas that can literally turn categories on their head. The secret, however, is often in the makeup of the teams that together make it happen. Internal teams and agencies usually have different skill-sets and the challenge is to fashion a unified team that is complementary, with everyone working together, a clear direction, aligned incentives and no politics.

Agencies work in a variety of ways with companies, including project by project and on an on-going, retainer basis, like an extension of your in-house team. Before you can figure out which way to go and who does what, you first need to determine your requirements. This goes back to having a clear understanding of your short, medium and long-term business objectives, and a translation of that business strategy into measurable goals. Knowing what you need to accomplish helps you figure out what you should do in-house, and what outside partners should take on. Many roles, such as social media management that used to be done by agencies, are now frequently in-house at companies. This is because the pool of experienced people who can perform this function, as well as the tools required, have become far more accessible. Other roles such as brand strategists or user experience architects are still so highly sought after that it is difficult for brands to attract good talent. And when they do they often don't have the constant stream of work to justify them as full-time hires.

AGENCY SELECTION

> **Don't buy an idea, buy the way an agency arrives at the idea.**

Once you have defined your needs, the next job is to source the right agency. This is often a very ill-defined process, because companies don't do it very often. You can hire a sourcing specialist, known as a search consultant, or you can do it yourself. If you do it yourself, you should start with an initial list of 8–12 agencies. Google searches for agencies with experience in your category or industry can be useful as well as suggestions from your staff and network. Do not, however, restrict yourself to just agencies with direct experience in your category. Many of the behavioral dynamics of marketing and selling are consistent across industries.

> **To agencies with the right process, what is really important is buyer psychology and buying patterns.**

Also, brands often need fresh ideas which may be harder to get from agencies that are too rooted in a single category. Fresh perspective, informed by ideas from out of your category, is often just what a brand needs to break through.

Once you have your list, step one is to evaluate all your candidates against your requirements. This is the **RFI** (request for information) stage. Agencies submit their **RFI** response and from those you select three to five finalists for the final round. Once this is complete, you may want to visit the agency and see what the chemistry is between your team and their team. If you are looking for a long-term partner, this is vital. Finally, you ask the remaining agencies to present their vision for your brand, or the project, in person.

Agencies are experts at presenting. Beware of agencies, however, that just talk about themselves. As wonderful as they are, in the end the challenge is about you. Look for how much they have tried to understand your business, how much research they have done for their presentation and what insights they may have been able to discover, even without your input. Gauge them not only on what they might suggest, but more importantly on how they came to those recommendations. How they think will be very revealing.

> Being able to synthesize the complexity of the marketplace and rationalize strategy and tactics through a disciplined process is essential.

Hopefully, they will outline how they would approach the challenges of your business, what they would do and how they would do it. If they produce spec creative (for which you will need to pay something if you want to own it), remember that in most instances it will be fairly uninformed because they will not have done the work to develop strategic insights.

REACHING FOR THE STARS

> Smart, creative professionals will work their hearts out for clients who believe in them.

Getting the best out of your agency partner becomes the next challenge. To some that means getting as much work as possible for as little as possible, squeezing every drop of creativity and energy out of the agency before you drop them and move on to another. If you detect a bit of angst here, it is because all agencies have had clients who thought this way. The truth is, however, that smart, creative professionals will work their hearts out for clients who believe in them, but they will not respond well to abuse or lack of respect. This affects the quality of work more than the quantity. As Leo Burnett said, you want your agency team reaching for the stars.

Managing your agency with clear expectations tied to specified performance metrics as well as clear, open communications is the way to start a relationship. A good agency will have these processes in place, which will protect everyone and give you both shared goals. The tighter and more measurable they are, the better the outcome will be.

> Being responsive is key to your success, so educate your organization to support that responsiveness internally and with your partners.

Many agencies, even a few of the largest, can often move faster than their clients. This is a good thing because it means they can often get a lot done and have a big impact in a short time, which is usually what you want. Marketing today requires speed to adapt to changes in consumer behavior, moves from the competition, and other market developments. But many companies put up so many roadblocks, committees and approvals in the way of getting work completed that nothing much ever gets done. We have had clients who have invested extensively in our services only to have nothing to show for it because they couldn't make choices. Remember, agencies are a way to skirt the risk-averse cultures that many organizations have. Your job is to clear the way to success by minimizing the number of chefs in the kitchen and keeping the number of approvals to just what you really need to get things done.

There are many different sizes and types of agencies as previously noted. Some are only a couple of people and others have thousands of employees. It's worth considering this for a moment. The large, international agencies and those owned by the big agency holding companies tend to be high overhead organizations that are set up to work with very large budgets from large brands. This means that smaller clients can get lost in the shuffle. Clients with comparatively small budgets usually get the least expensive, least experienced team, often people just starting in the advertising world. This may feel like a bait-and-switch after dealing with a very senior team in the pitch process, and it often is.

Many agency experts have noted that the perfect size for an agency is around 50 people.

For midsized clients, tiny agencies with just a few people, can also be a problem in that they do not have the team, capabilities, or processes to handle the variety or amount of work you might need. This leaves midsized agencies, from 30 to 75 people in size, with the sweet spot being around 50. Agencies of this size are usually a well-integrated unit with good, natural communications, few silos, and involvement of agency leaders. This is important because you want the attention of the senior team if you can get it. Leadership at midsize agencies is often every bit as good, if not better, than at the big agencies; they are also a lot more available.

Agencies, if hired and managed well, can be a great asset. They can bring marketing expertise, capabilities, and experience that few companies can be expected to have, but that are absolutely necessary to succeed in the new marketplace. They can also bring people with a level of creativity and strategic sophistication that usually only the biggest brands can attract.

7. CONTENT

FUEL THE SYSTEM

Content makes the system work.

With the right teams inside and out, integrated systems and supportive management, amazing things are possible. But just like gas in your car, you need to keep
your marketing system fueled at all times. Content in its many forms is what
rides on the rails of your system and creates every impression about your brand.

**Staying top-of-mind with prospects and customers
requires producing a constant stream of fresh content
for every interaction.**

Content is every image and word you present about your brand. However,
unlike the system it rides on, which changes infrequently, content often has
a very short shelf life. While your logo and slogan may last for a while, your
marketing communications need to be fresh and relevant every time you connect; tell someone the same thing you've told them before, and they will tune
you out.

UNDER THE SURFACE

**Your brand will be judged by the relevance, quality and
originality of what you produce.**

Content, as we've discussed before, is a huge challenge for organizations that
are built to do other things. If your organization is all about renting trucks, it's
unlikely it will be good at content creation. But content creation is so important that every company has to get it right. That means either hiring an agency with content skills or setting up an internal content creation organization.

The strategic work, which tells you what to make and why, is the part of content creation most often missed and perhaps the most important element.

This is not as simple as having the photography enthusiast on your team use his camera to make videos. Your brand will be judged by the relevance, quality and originality of what you produce. Relevance will come from the strategic work you do, which tells you what to say, when and how. This is the big part of the iceberg under the water, and what determines if content will work or not. When you consider the amount and variety of content that a modern brand has to produce, and that each piece has to be exactly right for the specific viewer at the moment it is being viewed, then you understand the importance of the strategic work that delivers those answers.

TALENT

Everything else being even, the team makes the difference.

Creative production quality is easier to accomplish today than ever. Cheap 4k cameras, easy editing, and graphics make creating high-quality video, for example, open to all. But you still need experienced, talented people behind the camera, writing scripts, composing photography, and designing the look and feel of the brand and its manifestations. Great talent in any industry is not easy to come by. Experienced, talented people produce ideas and excitement that just couldn't happen without them.

While it's easier to get first-class execution today, creating content that sets your brand apart and has emotional impact is harder than it's ever been.

Talented professionals look at the same picture everyone else does and see something entirely different. It's their passion, their creative intelligence and the unique way their experience has shaped them to interact with the world that produces their originality. Consider that last terrible movie you saw. In all probability, they had all the same equipment and capabilities that the last excellent film you saw had. The difference inevitably was in the people using the equipment, and the quality of creativity and originality that they brought to the work.

STANDING OUT

The only successful recipe continues to be relevance, quality and originality.

Compounding this content challenge is the deluge of content in circulation. It seems since the cost of digital cameras and editing has gone down every brand and every consumer in the world is producing and posting videos. The sheer volume makes it harder to stand out and confirms that the only successful recipe continues to be relevance, quality and originality. In times gone by, when ad agencies were set up to produce TV commercials a couple of times a year, the average budget would be in the hundreds of thousands of dollars, and each production would be months in preparation.

The pressure to produce a great deal of content at low cost and to keep the system fueled makes the work that much harder.

Today, content needs to be just as good and produced much faster and more frequently for much less money. That requires new production models. Content creation teams need to be able to produce an ongoing stream of original, relevant, quality material, quickly and cost effectively.

WORKING TOGETHER

Marketing and IT need to work together seamlessly.

In the recent past, companies frequently left direction and management of all things involving digital technology to the IT department. This made sense in the days when companies were building their ERP systems, structuring complex supply chains and introducing new technologies. But as technology has matured and the battlefield has moved to consumer experience and the marketing arena, it has become more important than ever for marketing to lead the management of marketing technology systems.

> **The prime responsibility for the digital systems that interact with consumers has shifted into the marketing camp.**

The prime responsibility for the direction of the digital systems that interact with consumers has shifted into the marketing camp. That's not to say that IT's role in protecting data, privacy and system integrity is anything less than it has ever been; it just means that the IT department, as it works with marketing, needs to recognize that speed, flexibility and competitive responsiveness are critical attributes of winning in today's hyper-competitive environment.

8. CONSUMER-CENTRICITY

A NEW FOCUS

> **The days of the product-centric organization are over.**

Succeeding with the modern consumer requires that companies make the shift from a product-centric culture to a consumer-centric culture, if they haven't already. This means a real change to your culture to put the consumer at the center of everything.

We mentioned earlier how agency cultures are often very different from those at their clients. While some might think those differences might be about pool tables, skateboards, and massages, they really come from all the ideas that ladder up to your brand (Chapter 2). As you attempt to turn your company into a consumer experience–oriented organization, as described throughout this book, the cultural shifts required can become your biggest stumbling blocks.

> **Any orientation that is less than 100% focused on consumer satisfaction works against you.**

This not only requires the latest systems and a talented, dedicated marketing team, but also a new focus from every employee in your company. Anyone who in any way interacts with consumers on behalf of your company is critical, but all the other employees behind the scenes are important too. All of this takes strong leadership from the very top. No organization likes or wants to change, but armed with a clear vision and mission, and with consistent communication and shared experiences, any organization can change and achieve great things.

ONE DIRECTION

Harness the passion and energy of your team and anything is possible.

To begin with, every employee needs to understand what your company stands for, its purpose and mission. As we discussed in Chapter 2, they need to understand the company values that everyone should live every day, the essence of the brand and the pillars it is built on. They need to be able to explain the brand simply if asked and know what they do can help strengthen it or diminish it. If employees have a clear understanding of the brand mission, bringing the brand to life for consumers in every interaction will happen naturally. Of course, you will need guidelines and style guides, training and ongoing communications keeping it top-of-mind.

If your people can see how what they and their teammates do fits into the plan, they will be more likely to enthusiastically support it.

Many books have been written about creating and managing cultures in companies, but with the shift to the new battlefield of consumer experience, it is urgent that companies get everyone on board and rowing in the same direction. This doesn't happen on its own and needs to be a conscious effort from the top, which is then built into the procedures and processes of the company, including how individual performance is evaluated.

SHIFTING MIND-SET

It's harder to change old thinking than to change old methods.

In our experience, companies that have successfully made the shift from a product orientation to a customer orientation have not done so accidentally. Invariably it requires changing the focus from the company offerings to the needs of the consumer. While the marketing team may do this naturally, many other departments may not. Organizations will tend to be most comfortable doing things the way they always have, and changing the mindset to a consumer orientation may upset many long-standing procedures.

The tech pieces of the system are more accessible than ever. But getting the right people is still a challenge.

Change to a consumer-orientation:

- Needs leadership from the top.
- Customer orientation becomes an essential brand value.
- Instead of reaching out to customers whenever you have excess product or need sales, you now only reach out when a customer has a need or when you can provide a value.
- Product development is done in conjunction with your customers.
- Distribution choices are determined by what provides the most convenience and value to your consumers.
- Customer service and marketing communications are prioritized.
- The organization invests in the technology and people that will enable teams to super-serve customers.
- Personas are developed and shared widely in the organization.
- The company sets company-wide consumer satisfaction goals.
- Key metrics like Net Promoter Scores are gathered consistently and acted on.

- Every employee is recruited to support the brand's message in person and in social media.

- The organization invests in comprehensive consumer metric tracking and analytics.

EMBRACE CHANGE

Change always brings new opportunities and new ways to win.

Change is, of course, a constant. By the time you have reached this point in this book, the marketing world you were living in when you started reading may be different. This might mean that many of the strategies in which you have invested need to be tweaked, rethought or even thrown out. Don't be alarmed, this is the just the constant process of change that should be every company's friend. That's because change always brings new opportunities to do things differently and new ways to succeed. An organization that embraces change and makes it part of its culture will weather the storms of innovation and competition well. This means the courage to take smart risks, to do what is most right, not what is least wrong, and to be true to your mission. But just like a person weathering the storms of life, a company needs to have a solid, strong, immovable center. This is the underpinnings of the brand, the values, purpose, mission, and clarity that define a company's place in the world. Companies which have done the work to know the difference between what can change and what should not, and then have the integrity to stand by those choices, will do well no matter what the future holds.

A great product, a consumer-oriented culture, a strong brand, and a modern marketing system should give your company the advantages it needs to succeed.

Hopefully, this book will help you chart the right course for your company as you navigate the unpredictable waters ahead. While innovation will constantly shift the pieces on the board, and introduce new ones, the ideas we have outlined here should be relatively timeless until the next paradigm shift. A great product, a consumer-oriented culture, a strong brand, and a modern marketing system, should give your company the advantages it needs to succeed. You'll need a little luck too, of course, although as Jim Collins in *Great by Choice* says, you can influence your return on luck considerably. His research shows that companies and people seem to experience about the same amount of good luck and bad luck. The difference between winners and losers is that winners always have a way to survive through the bad luck until the next stretch of good luck arrives, which might be a good subject to explore next time.

ABOUT THE AUTHOR

Tony Quin is the founder of SoDA (the Society of Digital Agencies), a global association of leading digital agencies. He also founded IQ Agency, an award-winning marketing and advertising agency. Born and educated in the UK, Tony began his career in advertising at Leo Burnett and then moved on to direct television commercials and produce TV shows, before returning to his roots in advertising. Tony's work has included ground-breaking digital marketing and advertising, which has won the Grand Prix at the Cannes Cyber Lions as well as dozens of other awards.

www.linkedin.com/in/tonyquin

Press